The Church of the
3rd
MILLENNIUM

Living in the Spirit
and the Power of the Elijah Years

Marc A. Dupont

Revival Press

An Imprint of
Destiny Image® Publishers, Inc.
P.O. Box 310
Shippensburg, PA 17257-0310

ISBN 1-56043-194-6

For Worldwide Distribution
Printed in the U.S.A.

This book and all other Destiny Image, Revival Press,
and Treasure House books are available
at Christian bookstores and distributors worldwide.

For a U.S. bookstore nearest you, call **1-800-722-6774**.
For more information on foreign distributors, call **717-532-3040**.
Or reach us on the Internet: **http://www.reapernet.com**

For further information write:
Mantle of Praise Ministries, Inc.
272 Atwell Drive
Toronto, Ontario Canada M9W 6M3
FAX (416) 674-8465

Dedication

This book is dedicated to the past and present board members of Mantle of Praise Ministries—men and women who have wholeheartedly loved, accepted, and greatly encouraged Kim and me. To Mark and Dave Hoffman who gave us much-needed acceptance and friendship, and a spiritual home during our wilderness years. To Lloyd and Sheri Frazier who gave us much love and encouragement to press on. To Ron and Caroline Allen who have continually shared with us not only their wisdom but, more importantly, their hearts. To John and Carol Arnott who greatly encourage us by being both risk-takers for the Kingdom of God and wonderful messengers of God's grace and compassion to the Body of Christ. Especially, I would like to thank John Ruttkay, who helped me keep my sanity during the Eighties with his balanced discernment and a truly unique and vital sense of humor, which helped keep things in perspective.

Most of all, I want to express my thanks to my wife Kim, a board member of Mantle of Praise, and my main encourager for the last 13 years. She has selflessly encouraged me to go forward, often when she has not really understood where we've been or where exactly we're going. She has been relentless in her encouragement to have faith and to trust God not only during the easy times but especially during the difficult times. She has always believed that I possess certain gifts, even when they often seemed dubious at best to me. As Proverbs 18:22 states, I knew I was in God's favor when she came into my life.

Finally, I dedicate this to the King of kings and Lord of lords: Jesus Christ, the Lamb of God and the Lion of the tribe of Judah. Thank you, Jesus, that You not only desire to bring me truth and compassion, but to top everything off, You desire to be my best friend! Thank You for these days, and that You saved the best for last. May Your glory cover the earth as the waters do, and even more so!

Contents

Endorsements

"Marc Dupont is not just a teacher; he is a prophetic teacher with a heart for revival. Sensing ahead of time what the Spirit is saying to the Church, Marc delivers the passion of a prophetic revivalist with the experience of a pastor/teacher. Knowing Marc as I do, I highly recommend reading *The Church of the 3rd Millennium.*"

Wesley Campbell, founder
New Life Vineyard Church, Kelona, B.C., Canada

"Marc's collection of prophetic insights helps to map the spiritual horizon before us. May the revelations that this dear brother has received move from God's heart, through his, to yours, 'that the whole earth be filled with the knowledge of God's glory as the waters cover the sea.' "

Dr. Guy Chevreau, author
Catch the Fire

"Marc Dupont has deep yet fresh prophetic revelation that edifies the Church in its earnest quest to be wholehearted lovers of God. He has an excellent spirit rooted in genuine humility. Bless you as you take and read this book."

Mike Bickle, senior pastor
Metro Christian Fellowship, Kansas City, MO

Foreword

One of the greatest tensions for the Church in our day is that of grace versus law. All too easily, we can move out of a loving, serving, and thankful posture into one of contending with one another over doctrinal issues and matters of practice. It seems that we would rather cling to traditions and hold on to familiarity, rather than follow the Lord into new and unfamiliar territory. Every time God touches His people in an unusual way, we feel obligated to "take sides" and part the Red Sea anew. All along, the Father has simply wanted us to follow His Spirit right down the middle to possess His promise.

In the past few years, our heavenly Father has powerfully touched and transformed many lives, and attracted international attention in the process. Members of His Body have labeled His visitations variously as blessings, outpourings, renewals, revivals, distractions, or even (as risky as this may be) demonic manifestations! Two things at least are clear about it all: Lives have been changed for the good, and God seems determined to continue His communion with the hungry and humble despite critics and cynicism.

As never before, we are a fatherless generation that has never really learned where our boundaries lie. Perhaps these insecurities account in part for our fear of new things. Apart from a deep love for God, we would no doubt try to take advantage of His mercy. We little understand justice, let alone God's amazing grace and love. In our confusion, we tend to do what men do best: Fence out what we fear or don't understand, and erect a monument or memorial to what we feel we do understand. Unfortunately, what man feels he understands, man also feels he can control. This explains our natural gravitation toward orderly religion with fixed time and behavior boundaries. It also explains why every fresh move of God rarely finds ready acceptance or incorporation into our established religious patterns and organizations.

In this book, *The Church of the 3rd Millennium,* Marc Dupont brings us to understand the times and seasons in which we live, and the absolute importance of intimacy with God as a fundamental key to understanding and walking in His grace.

We live in perilous times marked by very few, if any, fixed foundations. Instability is the prevailing characteristic of virtually every aspect of Western society. Even the traditionally stable societies of the Near and Far Eastern nations are beginning to show cracks and crumbling from within. The Church of Jesus Christ is also in a season of transition, but God is behind this shaking—and for a very specific purpose. Only those flexible enough to follow "a cloud by day and a pillar of fire by night" will find their way. Long since the day Jesus died on the cross, those obvious outward signs and Old Testament methods of guidance are gone. They have been replaced by an inward witness of the Holy Spirit that is life-giving if followed, but disastrous if ignored. The Church of the third millennium must be a Church that is led by the Spirit of God, not by the flesh and minds of mortal men.

This prophetic book by Marc Dupont is a tool inspired and directed by the Holy Spirit to lead those "with eyes to see and ears to hear" into a new intimacy with their heavenly Father. I encourage you to read this book with your heart and spirit, not merely with your mind. Marc would be quick to tell you that the real author speaking between the lines is the Holy Spirit, who seeks only to glorify the Son and obey the Father. Let the Spirit illumine your life and guide you deeper into your heavenly Father's presence in the exciting days ahead in *The Church of the 3rd Millennium*.

John Arnott, senior pastor
Toronto Airport Christian Fellowship

Introduction

This book was never originally intended to be a book. It is comprised of the first nine or so newsletters written by me and sent out to some 300 leaders around the world. The purpose was not to try to come up with a book, but to help keep churches and leaders informed about what Mantle of Praise was involved with, and what I was currently focused on in my preaching.

As the early and mid-Nineties progressed, I realized that these letters were at least partially chronicling the core message of what I believed the Holy Spirit was wanting to say in those seasons to part of the Body of Christ. Not wanting to be presumptuous, I realize that it takes many unique people with many unique God-given perspectives to relate the whole of what the Holy Spirit may be wanting to say at any given season. At the same time, however, churches of many different denominations that I have had the privilege of being involved with have, at least to my face, expressed appreciation and gratitude for what little part of the overall perspective I have been able to share.

It is my hope that the people who read this will find a little bit of help in understanding some of the hopes and visions that the Lord Jesus may have been breathing on their own spirits during a crucial time of God "turning the tables" on our church order so that we might become more a house of prayer and less a well-managed religious program. It is also my hope that no one will read this and allow these words to direct his or her ministry. The purpose of New Testament prophecy is always to encourage, build up, and edify—never to control, condemn, or manipulate! The gift of life through Jesus Christ means, among other things, that as sons and daughters and fellow heirs we can all seek God and be led by His wonderful Spirit.

Two notes of apology: One, these letters were originally written for pastors and church leaders who have, or should have, a good, healthy knowledge of the Bible. Some readers might find themselves having to jump around in the Bible as they read some of the chapters because I have used many biblical passages to illustrate the things I believed the Lord was giving me to say. My general readership consisted of pastors and leaders who desired, and still desire, both to be led by the Spirit and to understand theologically why God is saying and doing the things He is doing. So, if you find yourself doing a lot of Bible page turning, I apologize, but it is always of great benefit to understand more of the Scriptures anyway.

Two, I am painfully aware that in my past letters there is a great deal of what can be called "prophetic pontificating." That is, heavy statements were made in such a way that it seems I am writing down or being condescending. That was not and is not my intent!

Thanks to John Sanford, I realize that there is a great deal of difference between preaching to a live group and writing a letter to an intelligent, God-seeking individual. I would have edited out all this, but then the book would not have been true to what it really is: the first nine newsletters covering what I believe the Holy Spirit was giving me to say. This is not to say that the Holy Spirit wants anyone to speak down to another. It is just that this is very much a collection of letters that are definitely dated.

If anyone is offended by some of those "pontificating" lines, I truly apologize. As stated earlier, New Testament prophetic ministry is not intended to control, manipulate, or condemn, but to encourage and exhort.

For the revelation awaits an appointed time; it speaks of the end and will not prove false. Though it linger, wait for it; it will certainly come and will not delay (Habakkuk 2:3 NIV).

Chapter One

The First Celebration
of the Nineties

At present, the Lord is seeing one crucial division occur among His people. It is not a division of doctrine about the Holy Spirit or eschatology, although we have certainly used these to create problems. Rather, it is a separation between those who are turning their hearts to the Lord and those who relish religion more than relationship.

Malachi, in prophesying about John the Baptist, said that in the spirit of Elijah, God will restore the hearts of the children to the fathers and the fathers to the children. During their ministries, both Elijah and John the Baptist had hard words for Israel. They spoke about the sovereignty of God over His children. The critical point of success for each of these prophets in serving God was seeing the people of God, in their hearts, come to a place of repentance. To be more precise, they aimed to see people begin to understand the Lord's complete sovereignty and to humbly yield to His revealed glory and absolute holiness.

Not coincidentally, the primary focus in the Nineties among many churches and denominations has been on intimacy with the Lord. Different labels and semantics are being used, but the bottom line is, the Spirit of God is drawing the hearts of the children of God to the Father. The teachings range from holiness to prayer, repentance, prophecy, etc., but people are beginning to hunger for more than just knowing that they are going to heaven; they also crave the "spirit of wisdom and of revelation" in the knowledge of the Father (Eph. 1:17).

Malachi stated that on the day the Lord of Hosts prepares His own possession, He will spare those who serve Him as sons (see Mal. 3:17). Internationally, much is happening now with the Kingdom of God compared to the prior decade. Even groups who deny that God speaks today believe we are in a special time frame. We are not just near the time of the Lord's return, but we are actually in the betrothal period spoken about in Hosea (see Hos. 2:14).

This is a time during which God has allowed His people to wander in the wilderness. Our pride, complacency, and unbelief that God can do something so much bigger than we have yet seen could keep us in that wilderness, unless we are renewed through intimacy with our Lord.

The good part of Hosea's story is, when Gomer fell into her old sins, God sent Hosea into the wilderness to find her again and to speak words of kindness to her. Then came a restoration complete with mercy, compassion, and provision.

The past 15 years have seen an exodus from the Church. The phenomenon of confused and frustrated church members has touched almost every part of the Body of Christ. Many church leaders during these years began to wonder if perhaps they were missing something, while others searched out new methods of church growth in an effort to stay current.

Often such leadership uncertainty has resulted in "train jumping." This is when a pastor or congregation suddenly changes programs or goals and attempts to duplicate the newest movement, but instead only succeeds in derailing the church and losing many members.

Other times, leaders have looked at church unrest and discerned it as rebellion, immaturity, emotionalism, or lack of faith. In light of this, it is important to remember that Jesus Himself, using a whip, drove the sheep and oxen out of the Temple. His disciples remembered later that it was written, "Zeal for Your house will consume me" (Jn. 2:17b NIV).

Jesus was not interested in people relating to the Father through a system. He wanted people who were zealous for God. If He had not driven those sheep from the Temple, they would have been sold for slaughter by a corrupt religious system. The same can hold true today for pastors with "sheep" and "oxen" in their care.

Vision

Proverbs says, when there is no vision or revelation the people are unrestrained (Prov. 29:18). Certainly the Western Church in modern times seems to be without restraint.

Whether you look at liberal interpretations, the quantity of blatant sin, or lack of unity in the Church, today's times are similar to when Israel had no king (see Judg. 17:6). For instance, the Bible says when there was no king everyone did what was right in his own eyes. And, again, when people were going out to the wilderness to hear John the Baptist (remember, Malachi referred to him as the spirit of Elijah), the message was given: "Repent, for the kingdom of heaven is near" (Mt. 3:2b NIV).

When the people of Elijah's time went to Mount Carmel, they repented of following false gods; then they declared, "The Lord—He is God! The Lord—He is God!" (1 Kings 18:39b NIV) They had come into a deeper revelation that the Lord is not just the Savior or Comforter, but He is God Almighty, and as such is King over everything.

Interestingly, the very name of Elijah means "the Lord is God." This is the essence of John's message: proclaiming the complete kingship of God over His people. But to get that revelation, people in the days of both Elijah and John had to go into the wilderness.

So how are we to think about vision? How are we to determine specific direction for our lives, especially now that so much is happening with the Kingdom of God?

Unfortunately, there has been a confusion of priorities. We have talked and taught that vision, or prophetic direction, is primarily for ministry or outward activity. Obviously, the Lord desires to give vision for extending His Kingdom, but that is not the chief purpose of the Lord's desire to communicate with us.

When we as human parents rejoice because our children are born with healthy eyes and ears, it is not so they can go out and make some money or enter the family business. We are glad because our children will easily be able to learn to communicate with us. And it is a great day when a child can verbally identify us as his mother or father.

For the same reason we rejoice over our children's development, the Father desires His children to have eyes to see and ears to hear—so we might know Him and, as good children, learn to imitate Him.

Jesus said He could do nothing on His own initiative, but He only did what He saw the Father doing (Jn. 5:19-20). Paul prayed for the church at Ephesus, that the Father would give it a spirit of wisdom and revelation in the knowledge of Himself. Paul continued in his prayer, that the eyes of the Ephesians' hearts would be enlightened to know the riches of their inheritance (see Eph. 1:17-18).

What inheritance? The inheritance that they now had as sons of the living God. In Romans, Paul says that the sons of God are led by the Spirit of God, and we have received a spirit of adoption or sonship. Therefore, we may freely cry out to Him "Abba" or "Papa" (see Rom. 8:14-15).

When Jesus addressed the lukewarm church at Laodicea (which is symbolic of the Church today), He promised to give it gold refined by fire (see Rev. 3:18). This brings us back to Malachi. When Malachi prophesied of the time of John the Baptist, he began by speaking of a period of undergoing the "refiner's fire." It is to be a time of purifying when no one is able to stand (see Mal. 3:2).

This is the fire Jesus advised the church of Laodicea to buy. Jesus quoted the prophet Isaiah, who said to the people of His time, "...Ever hearing but never understanding...ever seeing but never perceiving. For this people's heart has become calloused" (Mt. 13:14-15a NIV).

The NIV translation uses the word "calloused." Certainly, the Church of the Western world today is a calloused Church. Not only are we often lacking in compassion and real love, but our motivations seem to come more from the world's value system than from the Kingdom of God. Jesus said we should not be like the people of the world who seek first after money and materialism.

Why, then, is there so much teaching on prayer that focuses on getting a hold of the goods of this world? Instead, Jesus said that our Father knows we have need of such things, but we must seek first the King and His rule.

The word *calloused*, according to Webster's Dictionary, means "hardened and thick-skinned." This works both ways: Not only are we in the Church often insensitive to the needs of those around us but we also tend to be hard of hearing when it comes to the Holy Spirit. Some would say, "The gifts are working so we must be hearing from the Holy Spirit," but Jesus said there would be those who would prophecy, cast out demons, and heal the sick in His name, but He would not know them.

It is also not enough to have a good Bible knowledge or theology. Jesus said to some of the leaders of His time, "You search the Scriptures, because you think that in them you have eternal life; it is these that bear witness of Me" (Jn. 5:39). It is also possible to have a good testimony and still miss out. For example, in the parable of the ten virgins, five were locked outside the wedding party, not because they had lost their testimony but because they did not really know the bridegroom.

Joel 2:28 makes two basic observations about the end-time outpouring of the Holy Spirit:

First, the Lord will reach out to all of mankind. Undoubtedly, we are in a time frame today when that is beginning to happen; for from the Amazon Basin to the unreached peoples of the Soviet Union, the Kingdom of God is spreading across the globe at an unprecedented rate. Even among the Muslim peoples in Africa, conversions to Christ and signs and wonders have dramatically increased.

Second, the people of God during these times will be people who have eyes to see and ears to hear. I believe Joel speaks of a people who, rather than solely experiencing Pentecostal or Charismatic phenomena, will be like Jesus and attempt to do the things they see the Father doing.

The last two generations in the Western world have seen a radical breakdown of the family unit. One of the chief problems has been a loss of true father figures. Too many times the fathers' love is not rooted in commitment and intimacy with the children. In addition, the authority level usually is either nonexistent or abusive.

This syndrome has naturally led children to rebellion and confusion concerning identity and values.

This state of problems has also affected church structure and leadership. Many Christians, while clinging to their salvation and Christian ethics, have a very real problem with spiritual authority in their lives. The situation is often compounded when leaders in a church also have deep-rooted problems with authority. This results in leaders who, because of personal insecurity, compensate by heavy-handed control.

The worst symptom of the overall problem is that Father God, the very throne and authority of everything, is ignored and the Church too much resembles a system, rather than a people who know and are led by the Spirit.

The last few years have seen the beginning of the things Malachi spoke of, at least symbolically. For many leaders there has been a real desire to learn to commune with the Father. Many are agreeing with Jeremiah 7:11: We have made the Church into a self-centered and self-promoting system; instead, it should be a "house of prayer" (Is. 56:7).

As many in leadership reach out to know the Father, the Father is revealing His holiness more clearly. This revelation brings about insight into our hearts and motives, so that we may see things as the Father sees them.

To lead us to another revelation of God's sight, First Kings 8:38 says when we pray we should individually be aware of the afflictions of our own hearts and spread our hands toward the Temple. This reaching for the Temple symbolizes coming with honesty before the throne of the Father. From such a posture, we develop humility. In the end, God is pleased, for Isaiah says the Lord does not look on the proud but on the broken and humble (see Is. 66:1-2).

The Prodigal Son

The Holy Spirit teaches us how to seek first the Kingdom of God in our hearts. The fruit of this is (agreeing with the elders in the Book of Revelation) learning how to throw down our crowns, egos, and ambitions before the throne of God and to worship Him with a renewed sense of His glory and holiness.

We can only achieve this understanding of His true nature when our gifts and ministries are renewed by the refiner's fire. We know they need refining because our abuse of gifts in the world is wasteful, and our abuse of spiritual gifts is sinful. In fact, many are learning from the Holy Spirit that even though good things may have been happening in our ministries in the name of Jesus, we have not necessarily been doing those things from pure hearts.

The refiner's fire of Malachi 3 that purifies our hearts, or buying gold like the church of Laodicea (see Rev. 3), is not an easy or light thing. It costs everything. Consequently, we find it difficult to die to self. The end result for many as they come to the Father is they settle into a slave's attitude: "Now all I want is to be a slave to you, God, and to receive a slave's portion."

This is how radical the Holy Spirit's revelation is. It is a revelation of the Father and His throne that makes the value of everything else, especially personal glory, fade away.

The good news is that traditionally this is exactly how the Lord works. Indeed, the most basic of all patterns with the Lord is that when we repent, He always responds with mercy and grace. As we begin to identify with the prodigal son, the Father is free to draw us in as sons.

This is a time of incredible celebration for many who have been truly seeking the Father. It is a celebration ordained by God and anointed by His Spirit. In such a season of homecoming, the Father bestows five distinct blessings on His prodigal children.

First, He folds us in an embrace and bestows a kiss. The embrace symbolizes complete acceptance into the household as a son. The kiss symbolizes the Father's desire for us to intimately know His love.

Second, He covers us with a robe. More than ever, many will find in this season they have a greater covering and protection over their lives in the areas of temptation and spiritual warfare.

Third, He gives the ring, which signifies greater power and authority in prayer and ministry. We will experience this power and authority when we comprehend what Jesus meant, "Pray to the Father, in My name." He never meant this as a formula, but He wanted us to understand that we should learn to communicate with the Father. He desires that we know His voice and also that to pray in Jesus' name means our hearts should be motivated like His—to want to please the Father, no matter what the cost.

Fourth, He shods our feet with sandals. Sandals, shoes, or the feet are quite often biblical symbols of the gospel or of being a messenger of the good news. In this time of homecoming, many Christians will wear their good news sandals and see the Kingdom grow in people who were previously far from the Lord. Not everybody will be an evangelist, but there will be a greater freedom to communicate the Lord to people as we ourselves learn to trust and submit on a deeper level. As a result, many churches will experience "end-time fruit" in their ministries. They will begin to sample the end-time moving of the Holy Spirit in a sovereign way.

Also, I believe there will be a great move toward unity in the Body of Christ as we begin to realize the Father's guideline: "Perfect love casts out fear" (1 Jn. 4:18).

Last, the fattened calf symbolizes the party the Lord wants us to experience. For many of us, it seems hard in this day and age to relate to the joy of the Lord. It is difficult to be happy during grim years, but in this season, the Father is going to celebrate the "homecoming" of many of His sons who have been out doing their own things.

One pastor of a mid-size church fits the picture of what I have been describing here. The Lord had allowed him and his church to go through a death process over a couple of years, even as they earnestly sought after the Father. At the end of the two years, I attended a seminar in this church entitled: "What the Father is saying."

On the last day of the seminar, the Lord had me prophesy the following over the pastor:

"Now the Lord is welcoming you home as the prodigal son. This is a year of new acceptance from the Father. The worldly rebellion you brought into your life with God is now broken. You and those around you, the church, are going to have a special year of celebration and harvest."

On the following Monday, the pastor contacted me and related that on Sunday the Holy Spirit had come over the church in a radical way. He said he had never before seen such a powerful freedom for worship and celebration.

When he told me this over the phone, the Lord spoke to me and said this was the Father's homecoming party for that church and that the fattened calf was being prepared.

In a unique way, this story is an example of the larger Church. The Father is really drawing the hearts of His children to Himself. The Lord, along with the multitude of angels, is joyfully preparing a party for the children who are responding to His invitation. He is preparing for the great harvest to come.

Chapter Two

Mounting Up
With Wings of Eagles

Intimacy with God is the challenge facing the Church today. Isaiah 40:31 powerfully speaks about the strength a close relationship with the Lord brings: "...those who wait for the Lord will gain new strength; they will mount up with wings like eagles, they will run and not get tired, they will walk and not become weary."

Of course, Isaiah is making an analogy here, but, nonetheless, he is speaking about the possibility of a fuller experience of knowing and serving God. In general, when we look at the evangelical Church today, we see few people who continue to walk and not grow weary, let alone many whose lifestyles reflect knowing and experiencing the fullness of the Spirit.

Isaiah, when prophesying that the Holy Spirit's fullness would be on Jesus, said Jesus would wear a "mantle of praise" instead of a "spirit of fainting" (Is. 61:3).

Regrettably, the Western Church tends to be dressed in the latter.

This is reflected in the quantity of "quick-fix" books in Christian bookstores. These books somehow impart head knowledge of the fruit of the Spirit, but they do so without taking people through the experience of walking and being filled with the Spirit. As a result, readers fail to be challenged to obey what the Lord is saying on a personal level.

What the Lord is saying at the close of this century ought to serve as a radical wake-up call. The Church would no doubt respond except for the tremendous paradox facing it: Wholesale pride, complacency, and weakness are rampant in the Church; meanwhile, God's call has been placed on the Church to demonstrate His Kingdom.

Coming into the last days—when the Spirit of God will rest on young and old, rich and poor, when young men will prophesy, old ones will dream dreams, and men and women will see visions (see Joel 2:28)—we are a people who have that spirit of fainting. Instead of changing from glory to glory, we are often a people who go from frustration to frustration, our lives being governed more by trials than by the Spirit of the Lord God.

Discerning the Signs of the Times

The disciples, whether they were cognizant of it or not, were caught up in a time frame pivotal for all humanity. Jesus said to them, "...many prophets and righteous men desired to see what you see, and did not see it; and to hear what you hear, and did not hear it" (Mt. 13:17). The ways in which Jesus, the Messiah, moved throughout Israel were so revolutionary, not even the religious leaders, who should have known what was happening, were prepared for Him.

This radicalness of Jesus was not a religious fanaticism or a legalistic austerity, but a complete demonstration of two things: the authority of the Kingdom of God, and the heart of the Father. For that reason Jesus admonished Philip that if he had seen Jesus he had seen the Father.

Coming into the present, we also live in a time frame that, though not the pivotal time of the cross and resurrection, is, in fact, a historical time, a time when the Spirit of God is moving on humanity like never before. It has been said there have been more people coming to Jesus as Lord and being filled with His Spirit in the last 20 years than in the previous 2,000.

In the early Nineties, the pace of the Kingdom quickened. Many nations in which the gospel has not moved for decades or centuries are now opening up, especially in the Muslim and Third World nations. When we look at things Jesus spoke of in Matthew 24 pertaining to the last days, such as wars, rumors of wars, earthquakes, famines, and droughts, it is highly possible that we are either in the last days or coming into them very quickly.

One has only to take a cursory look around the world to see this. For example, catastrophic events are commonplace in Sudan and other parts of Africa where millions and millions of people starve daily. In Mozambique, one out of every three children never lives to his fifth birthday. In Bangladesh, in 1991, over 140,000 people died from flooding and a cyclone. The same year in Red China, there were millions homeless due to flooding that touched half the nation.

It is very easy to look at these tragedies, as well as the increase of hatred, sin, and violence in the world, and out of a motivation of fear, pray for the return of the Lord. This was the case during the Sixties and Seventies when many ministries looked at the culture and said the Lord's return was imminent.

However, significant world events occurred in the ensuing decades, demonstrating God's mercy in tarrying. For instance, if Jesus had come before the 1990's, the Soviet Union, a nation of more than 290 million people, would never have experienced the incredible move of the gospel that is now being birthed all across the nation.

Again, God's mercy has been shown to Mozambique, which had had Marxist rule for over 20 years—complete with corruption, starvation, poverty, and persecution of Christianity. Today, the nation enjoys new freedoms, and the gospel is moving across the land at an incredible rate.

In Matthew 24:8 Jesus said that when these signs took place, they would be birth pangs of what is to come. Just as final labor pains for a pregnant woman are incredibly difficult to bear, the time comes when the baby emerges and the pain is forgotten over the joy of the child. Jesus said that during this time the gospel would be preached in all nations.

It is this time frame I believe we are witnessing—a time during which Joel said that the Spirit of God would touch all mankind. Joel prophesied of a time when, just as the Kingdom cut like a knife through Israel with Jesus, the Kingdom of God today, by the sword of the Spirit, shall cut through the whole world.

Who are the people who will wield this sword? It will be the young and the old, male and female, rich and poor. It will be the people who have eyes to see and ears to hear. It is going to be the people of whom Jesus spoke, who know Him not just as Savior, but as the Lord God Almighty.

That is to say, the people who are going to be effective for God are people who know in their hearts—not just in their heads—that Jesus is in the Father and the Father is in Jesus. People who in their attitudes and practices relate to life as though they are representatives not just of free fire insurance but of the King of the universe.

This is the King who said, "All authority has been given to Me in Heaven and on earth" (Mt. 28:18b). The people who follow this king will be the peacemakers in the huge harvest to come. They will be the ones who, because of intimacy with the Father, are led by His Holy Spirit.

These believers, as promised by both Jesus and Paul, will be known as the sons of God. They will do the things Jesus did. Being the people of whom Joel prophesied, they will see visions, dream dreams, and themselves prophesy. Because they are filled with the Father's love, which casts out fear, these will be the ones who are free to touch the world's cultures with the prophetic sword of the Spirit.

The Battle Call Is Sounding, But Where Are the Soldiers?

It is too easy in the Western Church today to be overfed, weak, and complacent. We often resemble spiritual couch potatoes, constantly entertained by vicarious Christianity. We can glibly sing "Onward Christian Soldiers" in our services, with false concepts of what it means to preach the gospel. Spitting out doctrinally correct rhetoric is not the same as ministering to people.

Not only have we failed with the gospel to have an overwhelming impact on the cultures of the last two generations, but even most church people are unable to relate to the world. We have become like the religious leaders to whom Jesus said, "...go and learn what this means: 'I desire compassion, and not sacrifice...'" (Mt. 9:13).

Those leaders spent hours and hours every day studying the Word of God, but they were without a clue as to the heart of the Father. In like manner, we are the last days' church of Laodicea (see Rev. 3:14). We think we are wealthy and have need of nothing, yet we do not understand how wretched, poor, blind, and naked we are.

The prophet Jeremiah asked the men of Judah, "If you have run with footmen and they have tired you out, then how can you compete with horses? If you fall down in a land of peace, how will you do in the thicket of the Jordan?" (Jer. 12:5)

This is a valid question for today. Jesus said that in the last days—the time during which the gospel will be preached to all nations—there will be tremendous demonic warfare against the people of God:

Then you will be handed over to be persecuted and put to death, and you will be hated by all nations because of Me. At that time many will turn away from the faith and will betray and hate each other, and many false prophets will appear and deceive many people. Because of the increase of wickedness, the love of most will grow cold, but he who stands firm to the end will be saved (Matthew 24:9-13 NIV).

We are at a time when both demonic warfare and the pace of what God is doing and saying are increasing dramatically. Already, because of pride and complacency, many ministries that in recent years were on the cutting edge of God's activity are no longer current. For many Christians who are not catching what the Spirit is saying, it will become increasingly harder to catch up.

Jesus says, "I am the gate; whoever enters through Me will be saved." But that is only half the verse. He continues, "He will come in and go out, and find pasture" (Jn. 10:9 NIV). This is hard for many people to relate to. What does Jesus mean "go in and out"? In and out of what? Is not the pasture in the sheep pen?

Of the first generation out of Egypt, only Joshua and Caleb entered into the Promised Land, because they were the ones who believed God could deal with the giants of the land. At a relatively advanced age, Caleb said he was still strong for going out and doing war and for coming in. When Caleb, at age 85, went out, he went to do warfare against the enemies of God. He went out and captured more territory for Israel. When Jesus ministered to the woman at the well, His disciples were amazed He would even talk to a Samaritan woman. A good and proper Jewish man would not do that. When they told Jesus they had food for the evening, Jesus replied, "I have food to eat that you know nothing about" (Jn. 4:32 NIV)

Too much of the Church today is like the disciples in that situation. The real food God has for us is learning how to give, instead of constantly taking and taking. We think the good grass is in the Church. But the harvest is outside, and the Lord is calling us to be like Caleb, to go out and do warfare on behalf of the Kingdom of God.

What Are We Living For?

Bob Dylan's song from the late Seventies, "Serve Somebody," relates that there is no middle ground—a person will end up serving either God or someone else. This is how it is in the Kingdom of God, especially in the last days' race of running with the Holy Spirit.

But often, when it comes to stepping out in faith, we resemble Saul when Samuel was ready to crown him as king of Israel. He was hiding behind the baggage (see 1 Sam. 10:22). In contrast, when the Lord was ready to raise up David, a man God said "had a heart for God," David did not even want to wear Saul's armor when facing the giant. All he wanted was the slingshot he had grown up with and a few rocks. David, because of his zealousness for God, was ready to go for it (1 Sam. 17:37-40).

But, like Saul, we are often loaded down with so much baggage that it becomes a trap for us and keeps us from being able to respond when the Lord wants to anoint us. Paul writes to Timothy, "Suffer hardship with me, as a good soldier of Christ Jesus. No soldier in active service entangles himself in the affairs of everyday life, so that he may please the one who enlisted him as a soldier" (2 Tim. 2:3-4).

When Jesus, in Matthew 6, contrasts serving the world's spirit with serving the Kingdom of God, He speaks about not getting caught up in the attitudes and priorities of world cultures. In the Western world today, everything possible and impossible is done in the continual quest to make life comfortable so that we might live a life of luxury. The hidden trap is that to obtain a Madison Avenue life, we become slaves to the system.

It is time for the Body of Christ to lose weight. It is time to disentangle ourselves from all the unnecessary baggage the world tells us we need, so we can run the race as if we want to win. This does not mean quitting jobs and neglecting responsibilities. But in the decision-making processes controlling our money and time, the Lord desires more governance over our hearts and motives.

A change of jobs or a promotion with more money is not always from the Lord, especially if it will dominate more of our time. Having a new car or a bigger house is not always the necessity we think it is, especially if it will control our checkbooks.

The Lord wants us to learn how to move in the Spirit. This involves more than going to Spirit-filled meetings. It also means being part of the move of God to set captives free and heal broken hearts.

Ministering to others will teach us that a lifestyle of giving ourselves to the world is better than a lifestyle of constantly focusing on our needs. For many this will mean doing things that, at this time, are not common in most churches.

One opportunity might be to go once or twice a month to poor areas and distribute food, share the gospel, and pray for the sick. Another might be to give up a yearly vacation—both time and money—to go on a three-week ministry trip to the Soviet Union or Nicaragua. For others, it might mean an opportunity to learn to live on God's economy—perhaps living on only 60 percent of their annual income so that missionaries might be financially supported.

The possibilities are as endless as the uniqueness with which the Lord has created us. One thing is definite: It is time to get free. It is time to start spiritually jogging and exercising because the Lord, in the outpouring of the Holy Spirit of which Joel speaks, is inviting us to be part of the greatest move of the Spirit the Church has ever experienced.

He is calling us to wait on Him, and to *know that He is God*. He is calling us to walk and not faint, to run and not be weary, and to prophetically mount up and see what the Spirit of the living God is doing.

In May 1991, I met a man in Gothenburg, Sweden, who exemplified both sacrifice and creativity in the love of God. He had already achieved moderate success in the business world, so he knew his possibilities for a successful career in making money; however, he walked away from that for a mobile, street-side hot dog stand and began to sell hot dogs in the prostitution area of the city.

He purposely worked nights, when the most traffic of prostitutes and street people flowed. Basically, he was doing on-the-job evangelism. He laid down a foundation of being open and friendly to the people on the streets, and relationships of trust began to happen.

Like Jesus, hanging with prostitutes, thieves, and tax gatherers, he was taking the reality of God's love to people who would probably never attend a church service. Because he had a hunger to evangelize and was also open to the leading of the Holy Spirit, this man was taking the gospel to a hidden people, a group untouched by the Church.

The Holiness of David

There has been criticism of this type of message, an argument that we cannot be super-spiritual people who are perfect. This is true enough, if we are speaking about legalistic perfection. But when we look at the history of God working with mankind, it is possible to have a Church that is hot rather than in the lukewarm condition of Laodicea. The early Church lived out an expression of Christ that carried on the works of the Lord in touching the culture powerfully, rather than just drawing forth theological symbolism from the miracles Jesus did in the past.

The fourth chapter of the Book of Acts gives this description of life in the early Church:

All the believers were one in heart and mind. No one claimed that any of his possessions was his own, but they shared everything they had. With great power the apostles continued to testify to the resurrection of the Lord Jesus, and much grace was upon them all. There were no needy persons among them. For from time to time those who owned lands or houses sold them, brought the money from the sales and put it at the apostles' feet, and it was distributed to anyone as he had need (Acts 4:32-35 NIV).

It should go without saying, this is a far cry from the state of the Church today, especially in Western world countries. The example of sacrificial money giving is very crucial, because a person's use of money is one of the key indicators of where his heart, or his treasure, is. There is no mention in the Book of Acts that the early Church lived in some sort of sinless perfection. They were not a church without problems but a church deeply caught up in a radical love affair with the Lord.

David, the first true king of Israel, was chosen by the Lord to replace Saul, the first actual king of Israel. He was preferred by the Lord not because of sinlessness; on the contrary, David committed major sins, such as adultery, murder, and sometimes disobedience against the word of the Lord. But God chose David because he was a man after the Lord's heart (see 1 Sam. 12:14).

The most important character trait about David was his love affair with the Lord. It was his treasure that neither moth nor rust could destroy and no thief could steal. Like challenging Goliath, his love affair was something worth dying for. It was a love affair of sometimes reckless abandonment.

At this time the Lord is wooing the Church in preparation for the wedding to come. Revelation 19 says this:

"Let us rejoice and be glad and give the glory to Him, for the marriage of the Lamb has come and His bride has made herself ready." It was given to her to clothe herself in fine linen, bright and clean; for the fine linen is the righteous acts of the saints (Revelation 19:7-8).

It is time for the Church of Laodicea to go through the fire and clothe itself in the white garments the Lord has prepared for us (see Rev. 3:18).

Chapter Three

Joshuas and Calebs for a Free Generation

If we think of revival not as artificial Church noise but as the Kingdom of God coming over cultural groups and nations, then we can think about it as a two-step process.

First, revival brings restoration to the Church. In fact, restoration is a more precise word to use than revival. Restoration means returning to its original state something of value that has become worn or blemished.

Second, restoration allows the outpouring of the Lord's compassion and reality on the general populace through the people of God. When we look at the restoration Elijah brought, followed by the ministry of Elisha, we see this scriptural pattern. It is repeated with John the Baptist's ministry, followed by the coming of the Lamb of God. Both of these examples had a great effect on the societies of their day. Another poignant example is in Psalm 51, where David recognizes that the fruit of his own restoration to the presence of the Lord would be sinners being taught of the Lord.

Today we are in a similar prophetic period, when God is preparing His existing Church for a huge explosion of the gospel. In many areas of the world, the Kingdom is tearing down walls of false gods. Part of being a prophetic church or person, however, is not merely hearing from the Father but being obedient and doing what He says.

Noah was not a prophet just because He knew what God was saying; he was a good prophet because he based his life, his hopes, and his dreams on preparing for what he believed God was going to do. As Church leaders today, it is not enough to be caught up in prophetic fervor, but we need to prepare for what God is going to do.

This means we not only have to recognize our need for being changed by God but we must also realize this change is to free us to love the Father first, as Jesus did. Then we must do what Jesus did in preparation for returning to the Father.

Jesus' death on the cross did not bring us the message of the cross. No, for not only did Jesus give His life for us but He gathered, taught, and trained disciples to start and lead His Church after His return to the Father. Much of His time was spent strictly with His disciples, disciples the Father specifically gave Him. Most of the time Jesus was not teaching and healing the multitudes; rather, most of the time He shared His life, His soul, and His love of the Father with a small group of men, preparing them to be leaders of His future followers.

Our human nature dictates that bigger numbers mean more success. Jesus, when preparing His disciples, worked on the premise that quality is better than quantity.

Jesus deliberately said things like,"He who eats My flesh and drinks My blood..." knowing that not only would the crowds be confused by this but many of His disciples would also leave Him, thinking Him insane (see Jn. 6:53-67). According to the apostle John, Jesus even asked His closest friends and disciples if they too were going to leave Him.

The point was this: At that time the primary thing for Jesus to accomplish, other than the cross and the resurrection, was to make disciples. But not just any disciples, for belief and obedience were not enough. He specifically prepared these 12 men to be the first apostles of His Church, which He knew would dramatically explode after Pentecost.

A Prophetic Generation to Kill Giants

As I stated in the previous chapter, the first generation out of Egypt never entered into the Promised Land. This was not because of Israel's sin with the golden calf, but because of their unbelief that God could take them into a land that was occupied by giant warriors who were much better prepared for war than the Hebrew men were (see Num. 13).

When the people wanted to stone Joshua and Caleb for telling them to have faith in the Lord's goodness, God judged Israel and swore that none of the generation over 20 years of age, except Joshua and Caleb, would enter into the Promised Land. All the others would die in the wilderness.

The writer of Hebrews says that the people hardened their hearts when they heard the Lord speak (see Heb. 3:7-11). By so doing, they provoked the Lord to judgment. The children of that generation, however, did have faith to respond to the voice of the Lord.

What was the difference between the first and second generation? They had both seen the miracles, signs, and wonders, not only in Egypt but in escaping Pharaoh through the Red Sea. They had both experienced the manna and quail from above and water coming out of rocks.

The difference was that this generation had grown up in freedom with God. As children, they had been used to seeing the Holy Spirit lead them, not only through Moses but being virtually tangible as a cloud of glory by day and a pillar of fire by night.

As the Holy Spirit is being poured out today, especially on the children and those beginning to relate to God as a child, a new generation is growing up. This will not be a generation of "church kids," but a generation that experiences the reality of a personal God who speaks and leads in a greater dimension than previously seen.

Like the younger generation that came out of Egypt, this generation will see the reality of what prophets like Joel and Habakkuk saw: the Spirit of God touching all mankind and the glory of God covering the earth as the waters do. This will be a generation that, because of its intimacy with the Lord, will have more faith in God's power to kill the demonic giants of the world's cultures than does the Church today.

Many Christians have more faith in the antichrist's power, and in satan's ability to threaten the Church, than they do in God's ability to touch the world in a powerful way.

Out of the Mouths of Babes and Infants

In recent years, the strongest moving of the Holy Spirit I have seen has often been with children under 10 to 12 years of age. From Nigeria to Indiana, Toronto to Norway, the Holy Spirit is coming on kids today very freely and powerfully.

Not long ago in Malmo, Sweden, while I was visiting a Christian school, the Holy Spirit began to fall on many of the students. There were several 12-year-old boys present who were not Christians. The Holy Spirit began to fill them as they opened up during the ministry time. I directed them to lay hands on one of their friends who was also present at the meeting and pray for him in Jesus' name.

As they were praying for him, he fell to the floor and collapsed completely under the power of the Lord. The two boys who had not yet surrendered their lives were in total amazement. Like with Peter at Cornelius' house, the Holy Spirit wants to fill people who are crying out for the reality of God. He will even use young children!

Lately, during meetings where the Holy Spirit has been falling, many of the most credible visions and prophesies I have heard have come forth from the mouths of children.

In Hammar, Norway, September 1991, a boy who was touched by the Holy Spirit was not experiencing any outward manifestations. But during the remainder of the day, he was unusually quiet and still. The next day he was back to his normal self. After dinner that evening, however, he said to his parents, "We need to pray more; we need to seek God together."

In Indiana, during a conference the previous year, we had a special prayer session for the children. We had prophecies for several kids around ten years of age, that the Lord was going to use them prophetically. Imagine my delight when the pastor told me that later in the afternoon and evening, one young boy in his congregation related several visions and words that he was receiving from the Holy Spirit.

These things happening with kids are not only important for their generation but they are symbolic for all of us. Malachi talks about how in the end times the hearts of the fathers will be restored to the children, and the hearts of the children to the fathers. Right now our heavenly Father is bringing restoration to the hearts of His children.

If the Lord is going to break down the barriers of Islam, Hinduism, Buddhism, and Materialism in the last days, the movers of the Kingdom will be those who—because they know the Father and what He is saying and doing—are not led by either fear or circumstances. The apostle Paul said, "...those who are led by the Spirit of God are sons of God. For you did not receive a spirit that makes you a slave again to fear, but you received the Spirit of sonship. And by him we cry, 'Abba, Father' " (Rom. 8:14-15 NIV). These will be the peacemakers who will be called "the sons of God."

Father Figures for a Prophetic Church

As the Body of Christ goes through the restoration years ahead and learns to be childlike, the Lord will establish father figures. Culturally, in North America and Europe, we are enterning the third generation in which the family unit is almost nonexistent. This is especially true of the present young generation, when more children are coming from broken families than intact ones. Because of the growing rampage of divorce, child abuse, alcohol and drug-diseased parents, and parents unable to understand their responsibilities, I am calling the up-and-coming generation the "fatherless generation." Even for the two previous generations, too many families have been actually dysfunctional, and children have grown up with warped perceptions of what it means to be parents. There is almost no understanding of what it means to set a real example of selfless love for children. Despite this grim reality, our confidence does not have to be shaken by the advancing ruin; instead, it can powerfully rest in the Father, who is "a father to the fatherless" (Ps. 68:5 NIV).

To a lesser degree, the same lack of selfless love has infiltrated the contemporary Church. There is no lack of gifted people in the Church today, but there is a definite lack of people prepared to give themselves to others as Jesus taught His disciples to do. As First Corinthians 4:15 (NIV) reads: "...you have ten thousand guardians in Christ, [*but*] you do not have many fathers...." Many people in leadership have a passionate abandon in their hearts for the Lord, but because they come from dysfunctional family situations, they cannot persevere in living out God's will for their lives.

It is not enough to say that we love God and are deeply committed to Him. John asked, "If we do not love the brother that we see, how can we love God whom we have not seen?" (See First John 4:20-21.) When asked the greatest commandment, Jesus did not just say the first, which is to love the Lord our God with all our hearts. He continued by saying that the second is almost the same in importance: to love our neighbor as ourselves (see Mk. 12:29-31). He demonstrated this by washing His disciples' feet, telling them that if they wanted to be leaders like Him, they would have to be involved in the lives (dirty feet) of His people.

This illustrates our point. Part of God's process in preparing the up-and-coming generation is to provide father figures. The problem is, how can we be fathers if we have not first learned to be real brothers with one another? And how can we be real brothers with one another if we have not first learned how to be childlike with God the Father?

So in preparing the Church for an explosion of the gospel, the Lord is making the foundation bigger and deeper. First, our relationship with the Father deepens in the intimacy discussed previously. Second, our understanding of what it means to have the Father's sacrificial love for people broadens.

So what is a scriptural "father figure"? In the contemporary Church, with its strong values of theology and authority figures, we might say a father figure is someone in his fifties, or older, who is still in active leadership and has been "successful" in pastoring or teaching.

But is this really all we need? If we look at the two older leaders of the Hebrews as they crossed over the Jordan, we see something a little more radical. If we look only at Joshua's and Caleb's gifting or trained skills, we get a methodological, patterned, or statistical type of sketch that might be interesting but does not really mean a thing.

The problem we have today in the Church is not so much a lack of gifting, as a lack of godly character. Usually when we talk about "godly character" in a person, we relate that to personal holiness, or a lifestyle filled with sacrifice. These things are certainly part of godliness, but they do not present a complete picture.

The outstanding thing we see in the lives of both Joshua and Caleb is risk taking.

Currently, there is an established pattern among today's leadership: Once success happens (relating to money and numbers), complacency and safety become more valuable than new breakthroughs in the Kingdom. Even leaders who may have begun their ministries out of radical obedience to the Lord become entrenched in conservative, "don't-rock-the-boat" tradition. Often tradition comes out of past obedience and becomes our present bondage. Basically, once one level of success is reached, the risk taking often stops.

God is an incredible risk-taker. When we cease to be risk-takers, we passively begin to settle into religious patterns rather than to be led by the Spirit of God. Whether He was creating man in the Garden of Eden, giving His only begotten Son on the cross, or turning the leadership of the Church over to the 12 apostles, God was and is an enormous risk-taker.

I do not mean by "risk-taker" someone who takes chances just for the sake of taking chances. What I am talking about is the difference between being religious and being spiritual. The prophet Samuel told Saul that God was not interested in his religious sacrifices. He said, "To obey [God] is better than sacrifice" (see 1 Sam. 15:22 NIV). Jesus told the Scribes and Pharisees that God was not interested in their sacrifices; instead He was after mercy (see Mt. 9:13). But the Scribes and Pharisees were too concerned about their reputations to take a risk and demonstrate God's mercy and compassion to prostitutes, thieves, and lowlife.

As time goes on, through the Nineties and beyond, God will call Church leaders to take more visible and costly risks. It will become more costly to be obedient to the Father in future years. Why? Because God is pulling out all the stops; His Kingdom is on the move, and like Jesus approaching the cross, our crosses are going to get bigger.

The Lord is going to force leaders to deal with their motivations. Are we living for the Kingdom of God or for the kingdom of man? Is our biggest concern the captives and the brokenhearted, or is it our reputations and "keeping the boat afloat"?

What was the difference between Joshua and Caleb and the rest of their generation? Numbers 14:24a (NIV) says this, "...My servant Caleb has a different spirit and follows Me wholeheartedly." Numbers 32:12 (NIV) says that none of their generation would see the Promised Land *except Caleb and Joshua,* "for they followed the Lord wholeheartedly." This testimony suggests that they were more than merely radical young men. When Caleb was 85 years old, he said to Joshua,

I am still as strong today as I was in the day Moses sent me; as my strength was then, so my strength is now, for war and for going out and coming in. Now then, give me this hill country about which the Lord spoke on that day, for you heard on that day that Anakim were there, with great fortified cities; perhaps the Lord will

*be with me, and I shall drive them out as the Lord has
spoken* (Joshua 14:11-12).

At his advanced age, Caleb was still a risk-taker. He
was willing to leave his prior successes behind and lead
the tribe of Judah into a new country, with new enemies. Why? Because he was still basing his life on what
the Lord directed him to do. He was still being led by
vision from the Lord, rather than by general principles
or merely good theology!

Fathers Preparing Children

At the beginning of this chapter, I said that Church
leaders today must go beyond being caught up in the
current prophetic fervor; strategically, we need to syn-
chronize our preparations with God's. What the
younger generation needs is visible, living examples of
mature, godly men in leadership who, rather than
maintaining the status quo, base their lives on the
Spirit's leading.

But part of this need transcends role models. As intimate relationships are developed, three things are im-
parted: character, love, and healing. Overall, the Church
leaders who emerge as time goes on are going to be,
more than anything else, real "father figures" who
closely take interest in what God is doing with the next
generation.

This is precisely what God is now doing. Jesus was
the perfect example, for in addition to fulfilling His
own ministry, the cross, He also prepared His disciples

for the day when the Spirit would fall and the Church would explode in growth.

Another example we have of the father figure model is David's relationship with his son Solomon. The time came when David prophetically realized that the Lord was not going to allow him to be the one to build the temple. (Interestingly, David found this out through prophetic ministry—namely through Nathan the prophet—rather than through his own wisdom.)

David was at the peak of his powers and popularity. It was his intention to build this magnificent temple as a place of worship for the Lord. But the most significant part of David's life was his intimacy with the Lord; so even though he was king, he backed off from his own plans and listened to what the Lord said. The Lord informed him that since his hands were bloody from being a man of war, he would not be the one to build the temple (see 1 Chron. 22:6-18). Whoever was going to build the temple would have to be a man of peace (see 1 Chron. 28:3).

This is exactly what God is bringing about in the Church today. Too much sin, warfare, and bloodshed exist within the Church because of leadership's rampant spiritual pride and heavy, self-righteous, judgmental attitudes. The Lord is raising up a generation of leaders who, as a result of intimacy with God, will walk in obedience and humility. These will be the peacemakers.

David was told by the Lord that one of his sons would build the temple. God said, "...I have chosen him to be My son, and I will be his Father" (1 Chron. 28:6 NIV). This, again, is a picture of what God is doing today as He builds up a generation of those who have a childlike relationship with God the Father. This will be the generation that, symbolically speaking, will build God's temple. As Habakkuk says, "For the earth will be filled with the knowledge of the glory of the Lord, as the waters cover the sea" (Hab. 2:14 NIV).

So rather than sit back and be content to continue on in the momentum of what God was already doing in his life, David began to prepare Solomon for the building of the temple. David gathered 1,000,000 talents of silver and 100,000 talents of gold. Then he gathered iron, bronze, and stone; carpenters, stone cutters, and ironworkers. He spared no expense because he considered it more important to bless what God was blessing than to do his own thing.

Three qualities are required for the type of leaders we need for the Church today. First, we need leaders who are absolutely committed to seeking first the Kingdom of God, rather than the kingdom of the Church or the kingdom of man. Second, we need leaders who are risk-takers—men and women who are not concerned about either their reputations or their own successes. These leaders will be like Jesus:

Your attitude should be the same as that of Christ Jesus: who, being in very nature God, did not consider equality with God something to be grasped, but made Himself nothing, taking the very nature of a servant, being made in human likeness. And being found in

*appearance as a man, He humbled Himself and be-
came obedient to death—even death on a cross!*
(Philippians 2:5-8 NIV)

Third, we need leaders who not only seek what God
is saying, but like David with Solomon, begin to prepare
the future generation of leaders for what God has in
store. Let us begin to focus on what God is doing in the
long run. And just as God is doing now, let us begin to
pour ourselves into the younger generation to prepare
them for building the temple. Let us equip a generation
of peacemakers who will be known as the children of
God. Let us forget about the status quo and let us, as Jesus said, "Permit the children to come to Me, and do
not hinder them, for the kingdom of God belongs to
such as these" (Lk. 18:16b).

*For the vision is yet for the appointed time; it hastens
toward the goal and it will not fail. Though it tarries,
wait for it; for it will certainly come, it will not delay*
(Habakkuk 2:3).

Chapter Four

Eating the Food Jesus Ate

...The hour has come for the Son of Man to be glorified. I tell you the truth, unless a kernel of wheat falls to the ground and dies, it remains only a single seed. But if it dies, it produces many seeds. The man who loves his life will lose it, while the man who hates his life in this world will keep it for eternal life (John 12:23-25 NIV).

Jesus spoke these words knowing He would soon be arrested, beaten, mocked, and crucified for a people who had and would again reject Him. When He was in the garden wrestling with His humanity, His singular focus on pleasing the Father made the difference in His decision-making process. What motivated His life and actions were His love for the Father and His desire to obey Him.

We are in a time today when the Father is preparing the Church for battle. The Captain of the Lord's Hosts is speaking to the hearts of the children, calling us into the Father's battle formation, as when the Lord gave

Joshua a strategy of worship to bring down Jericho (see Josh. 5:13-15).

The order and formation the Lord is establishing for the end-time Church is going to be prophetic. By that, I mean the Church will change from operating on human wisdom to operating on the wisdom gained from listening to and then obeying what the Lord has to say. It will not be an easy transition, for God's order is often contrary to our understanding and wisdom. This is because God's ways are above our ways and His thoughts are above our thoughts (see Is. 55:8). Too seldom, then, do we recognize that the beginning of wisdom is to fear God.

For many Church leaders, the Nineties will be a time of incredible upheaval. As Jesus cleansed the Temple, so God is cleansing us in order to make us into a house of prayer. The sacrifices of our works we bring into the temple are no longer going to be valued. This should come as no surprise, since many of us are familiar with Samuel's words to King Saul: "To obey is better than sacrifice..." (1 Sam. 15:22b NIV).

But do we really understand the effect of the forthcoming upheaval on our relationship with God the Father? The Bible promises specific rewards for those who remain faithful. Matthew 25, in the parable of the stewards and the talents, makes an interesting point concerning the master's rewards for obedience. The two stewards who had employed the talents given them were not only given more responsibility but were told to enter into the joy of their master. The shared joy was given as a reward for obedience rather than purely as a result of what the servants had accomplished.

Where Is Our Food Coming From?

In John, chapter four, the disciples returned to Jesus with food, but He told them He had food they did not know of. When they became confused, Jesus responded to them by saying, "My food...is to do the will of Him who sent Me..." (Jn. 4:34 NIV). He was telling the disciples what it was He actually lived on and what nourished Him.

The question for us is, what are we being nourished on? It is common to hear cliché proclamations such as "I am living to glorify my Lord Jesus Christ," or "I have received a manifesto from God to preach the gospel to the nations." To a certain degree, these types of statements sound very spiritual, especially when large sacrifices are made. But the question stands: Why are we doing what we do?

This question is important because the Lord is sifting hearts as never before. If God's hand is going to visibly increase in our lives, our hearts will have to be pure. Purity is essential because only the pure in heart will see God. It is possible to end up receiving our reward on earth, but to be bankrupt at the judging of the saints.

Too often, the pure in heart receive criticism from within the Church. For instance, when the woman washed Jesus' feet with costly perfume, the disciples were critical because the perfume could have provided a lot of money for the poor. On the other hand, the needs of ministry, just like the needs of the poor, are always with us, and God definitely wants us to be ministering His love and compassion to the world in practical ways. Still, as far as God is concerned, there is a greater priority than good works: The greatest commandment is to love God first.

Our love affair with God has to be the impetus behind our lives. Then from that love comes His perfect will revealed. This is what provides our direction and satisfaction.

Recently, while flipping through the television channels, I caught a few minutes of a show featuring a well-known Christian pastor and teacher. He was making final preparations for a spiritual warfare conference centered around prayer for a certain city. In a very theatrical style, he dramatically stated that God had created his wife and him for this particular last days' ministry.

Of course, God has ordained good works that we should walk in them, but this is not *why* He created us. God created us that we might know Him, love Him, and be loved by Him. There is a God-created hunger for Him within us that cannot be satisfied by anything but God Himself. Jesus is not *about* "the Life"; He *is* "the Life." Not even good works, as necessary and fulfilling as they are, can be a substitute for God.

Not by Bread Alone

Undeniably, for us in the Western world, our understanding of the Bible and of God is permeated by our culture's materialistic value system. We feed on numbers, outward success, and the accolades of man. Jesus, however, is quite unequivocal when He states:

> *Not everyone who says to Me, "Lord, Lord," will enter the kingdom of heaven, but only he who does the will of My Father who is in heaven. Many will say to Me on that day, "Lord, Lord, did we not prophesy in Your name, and in Your name drive out demons and perform many miracles?" Then I will tell them plainly, "I never knew you. Away from Me, you evildoers!"* (Matthew 7:21-23 NIV)

"Evildoers" here does not refer to overt sinners, but to those who practice Christ-like ministry without intimacy with God. That healings and deliverances take place is almost irrelevant. Jesus precedes this passage by qualifying what a true prophetic ministry is, and interestingly, He never says anything about whether or not the prophet is highly accurate. The point being, the obvious and the given cannot be used to determine success in the Kingdom, since God sees way beyond the outward appearances.

The question is, what is God really after in our service to Him? I am not trying to condone failure, laziness, or lame ministry, but I am saying that measuring success only by the yardstick of size and numbers can be very dangerous, if not demonic. Sooner or later, we need to come to the realization David did: The true sacrifice God wants from us goes way beyond money, time, or materialism. God desires truth in our innermost being, and that truth is Jesus.

If, through our cultural mind-set, we attempt to understand the gospel, then the goal of Christianity is reduced to nothing more than making it to Heaven and/or a position in ministry. Heaven becomes a home or mansion, and ministry is a position or title. In this realm, we work for money, which in turn allows us to purchase and possess things; for in our culture, success is measured by personal power and the quality and quantity of our possessions.

The problem is, if we do not experience the Father's heart, our personal identities and security continue to be controlled by what we can achieve, build, and obtain. With this mind-set, little is changed in our value process. We, perhaps, have changed ethics and morals, but we still operate from a value system in which bigger is better, and everything counts in large amounts.

Jesus, a master at parabolic teaching, said, "For where your treasure is, there your heart will be also" (Mt. 6:21 NIV). For the Christian, this statement is true not only figuratively but also literally. In spite of this truth, the world's continued influence can affect us, and our motivations can still be based on what we can accomplish, rather than focused on what God values foremost: our hearts.

We might actually be attempting to serve God, but be completely ignorant of what the Lord would like to say to us. Spiritual deafness can result if our hearts are focused on anything in Christianity other than God Himself. Frequently we ask one another, "What is the Lord saying to you?" We speak about the good things that are happening, but seldom do we tell what the Lord is actually *saying*. Frighteningly, we sometimes do this without even realizing we have not addressed the question.

In the final analysis, our motivation process has to change if we are going to continue on in the outpouring of the Holy Spirit. Because God gives grace to the humble, our motivations will change when we truly submit to God's sovereignty. This submission is vital because many areas of the world are already coming into times of God's sovereign movement.

Sovereign times refer to times when the Lord requires very little work from us, unlike times past when much work was required for a little harvest. It is like the second time when the Hebrew people had no water in the wilderness (see Num. 20). The first time, Moses worked a little: The Lord told him to hit a rock with his staff. But by the second occurrence, Israel had a deeper revelation of God and there was less room for man's efforts. Therefore, God told Moses just to speak to the rock. Ignoring God—for Moses preferred to operate from tradition—he hit the rock with his staff. God judged Moses, and he was not allowed to enter into the Promised Land.

God's call is to believe Him and to live by every word that proceeds from His mouth.

Coming to the Table With Jesus

In the Book of Revelation, chapter 3, the church of Laodicea symbolizes the Church today, the end-time

Church. We lean toward being lukewarm rather than hot, and prideful and arrogant rather than humble and compassionate. The Lord, however, as a loving Father, desires to heat us up. The fuel for the fire is intimacy with Him. Jesus finishes His rebuke of the Laodicean church with an invitation: "Behold, I stand at the door and knock; if anyone hears My voice and opens the door, I will come in to him, and will dine with him, and he with Me" (Rev. 3:20). The operative word is "hears."

It is not enough for Christian leaders today to recognize that we are in a prophetic time. Neither is hearing prophesies enough. The time is not just for prophets; it is for a prophetic Church. This is the latter fulfillment of the time Joel spoke of: "...Your sons and daughters will prophesy, your old men will dream dreams, your young men will see visions. Even on My servants, both men and women, I will pour out My Spirit..." (Joel 2:28-29 NIV).

Scripture gives a pattern of times when leaders were invited to sit and eat in God's presence. At these meals, revelation was the main food on the menu. Exodus 24:9-11 says:

> *Then Moses went up with Aaron, Nadab and Abihu, and seventy of the elders of Israel, and they saw the God of Israel; and under His feet there appeared to be a pavement of sapphire, as clear as the sky itself. Yet He did not stretch out His hand against the nobles of the sons of Israel; and they beheld God, and they ate and drank.*

Saul's history as king of Israel began with sitting down with Samuel the prophet and eating a reserved choice portion. Jesus told His disciples He had been longing to sit with them for the Last Supper. What was it that was really being served at these meals?

The outpouring of the Holy Spirit the world is now receiving is not just a release of power or anointing; it is God's manifest presence with us, the Immanuel. And as His presence increases in our lives and assemblies, the first real fruit is going to be humility, especially among the leadership. My friend Hans Lundahl, a teacher in Sweden, defines humility as being flexible. We must be flexible to the point that we are willing to bend and even abandon our own agendas so that we can do God's will instead of following our own presuppositions and traditions.

Walking With God

Both Moses and Joshua experienced just such an important turning point in learning flexible humility. Their pivotal moments came when they had direct encounters with the Lord. They came to an understanding that God is an incredible God who wants to do things His way. The one thing both Moses and Joshua experienced during these pivotal encounters with the Lord was this: They were told to take off their shoes because they were on holy ground—in the presence of the Lord (see Ex. 3; Josh. 5).

One reason God told them to take off their shoes was because He desired them to relax and to freely spend time in His presence. Like the invitation to the church of Laodicea, God wanted Moses and later Joshua to sit down with Him and spend intimate time together.

The Lord longs for us to learn to commune with Him and to enjoy His presence. David said, "Thou wilt make known to me the path of life; in Thy presence is fulness of joy; in Thy right hand there are pleasures forever" (Ps. 16:11). This is what Jesus meant when He said we should be called a "House of Prayer."

In Scripture, feet often symbolize taking forth the gospel. Paul exhorted the Ephesian church to put shoes on the feet of the gospel of peace. In an earlier instance, Isaiah 52:7 reads, "How lovely on the mountains are the feet of him who brings good news, who announces peace and brings good news of happiness, who announces salvation, and says to Zion, 'Your God reigns.' "

I believe the pavement of sapphire that Israel's elders saw under the Lord's feet in Exodus 24 is the "Highway of Holiness" described in Isaiah 35. Isaiah said fools would not walk on this highway. Now, Jesus told the disciples they were already clean because of the word spoken to them in John 13. But one area of cleansing evidently still remained: their feet. So at the Last Supper, Jesus stripped down to a towel and began to wash their feet. When Peter asked Jesus to also wash his hands and head, Jesus replied, "...He who has bathed needs only to wash his feet..." (Jn. 13:10).

Like the disciples, we too are clean because we have heard the word and have come into the Lamb's blood-cleansing. But our feet are dirty from walking by our own directions and from doing our own things, even if we have done so in the name of Jesus. The time is now here for us to walk hand in hand and heart to heart with the Lord.

...I will take hold of your hand. I will keep you and will make you to be a covenant for the people and a light for the Gentiles, to open eyes that are blind, to free captives from prison and to release from the dungeon those who sit in darkness (Isaiah 42:6-7 NIV).

To Whom Much Is Given, Much Is Required

The Lord is raising a new spiritual generation of leaders today. These leaders of the new wine will be flexible and humble, instead of stiff and proud. Without a doubt, prophetic times call for radical obedience.

This radical obedience is clearly illustrated in First Kings, chapter 13. The Lord sent a young prophet from Judah to Bethel. (Significantly, the root word for *Judah* means "deep celebration with praise and reverence to the Lord," and the word *Bethel* means "house of the Lord." These words are important for us today because restoration will originate out of our love affair with God.) But the young prophet, after obeying the Lord and bringing restoration to Israel, was then disobedient and took the advice of an older prophet and ate the food of man.

The older prophet had probably never seen the Lord moving so sovereignly and did not consider complete obedience a matter of importance. This disobedience cost the young prophet his life. Since he represented the sovereign King, sovereignty had to begin with him.

Today, before the return of our Lord Jesus, the Father is quite committed to reaching the multitudes with His love. Decreasingly will "churchianity" and spiritually void church practices be the norm. The King is on the move, and those moving with Him will need to be walking in revelation of the "I AM." Judgment is already on the Church, and it will increase throughout the next years. This is because prophetic revelation, especially about God, does not come without a stiff price tag.

In the late Eighties and early Nineties, the Lord dealt with hidden sins of the flesh and money, but now God is dealing strongly with hypocrisy and false motives. We must realize there will be consequences for these sins. Indeed, Jesus spoke about eyes to see and ears to hear when He said, "For whoever has, to him shall more be given, and he shall have an abundance; but whoever does not have, even what he has shall be taken away from him" (Mt. 13:12).

Anointing will increase greatly over the next several years, but for many, even what anointing and revelation they now have will be lost if they fail to respond to the Father's heart. Those who do not repent and return to their first love will lose their lampstands.

When Jesus criticized, it was not prostitutes, thieves, and outcasts He condemned. He condemned hypocrisy in the leadership. Soon, there will be nowhere in the Kingdom of God to hide. The day will come when the long list of people who are now in ministry will drastically change. Indeed God will remove some from leadership. The Lord, in His mercy, will take some home rather than continue to allow them to mislead His people, misrepresent His throne, and especially deny His heart.

Moses never entered into the sins of his fellow Hebrews. But like the young prophet in First Kings, his disobedience to what God had spoken to him cost him his life (see Num. 20:12). The Lord considered Moses' disobedience to His directions to be blatant sin. According to Numbers 12, Moses was the only man God spoke to openly, even mouth to mouth. God took this intimacy with Moses very seriously. To whom much is given, much is required.

Finally, it is imperative that we start listening to the Father and blessing what *He* is blessing, instead of continually asking Him to bless *our* plans and endless programs. But such listening begins and ends in our hearts. It is our love the Father is after. This is where our values and decision-making processes need to change. Then obedience out of revelation will follow. "...I tell you the truth, the Son can do nothing by Himself; He can do only what He sees His Father doing, because whatever the Father does the Son also does" (Jn. 5:19 NIV).

And, again, "...serve Him with wholehearted devotion and with a willing mind, for the Lord searches every heart and understands every motive behind the thoughts. If you seek Him, He will be found by you..." (1 Chron. 28:9 NIV).

Chapter Five

Love Versus Pharisaism

"...Destroy this temple, and I will raise it again in three days...," Jesus replied to His critics (Jn. 2:19 NIV). More than responding to the questions in the Temple, He was issuing a challenge to satan, not for the first time. Similarly, God said to satan, "...Have you considered My servant Job? For there is no one like him on the earth, a blameless and upright man, fearing God and turning away from evil" (Job 1:8).

In His sovereignty, the Father used satan to accomplish His perfect will with both Jesus and Job. In His infinite wisdom and love, God took the best He had and allowed satan to do his worst. Then, out of the ash heaps, God glorified His name. This is often His way.

In truth, it is the pattern of what is now coming upon the Church. As with Jesus, God is allowing the powerful spirit of Pharisaism to do its worst. The result will be a people who are broken and humble before God's throne, a people who will tremble at His word. The tables are being turned on Christians who have made idols out of theology, order, and tradition. Out of the confusion and desperation, a cry is coming for the reality of God's Spirit and love in the Church.

The ones who stand will be those who realize they are in a pit. The Lord will place their feet on the rock of revelation. The ones who endure will be the flexible, the humble, the ones who learn to pray, "Not my will, Father, but Your will be done."

Blessed are the flexible, for they shall bend and not be broken. But the stiff and proud will be spit out of the Lord's mouth.

We are quickly entering tremendous warfare that will devastate some churches so thoroughly that even the dust will be scattered. Others will be broken to pieces, but those pieces will be living stones, smooth and conformed to the person of Jesus. They will be stones that fit together and complement one another in unity, for building an end-time house of prayer. These workable stones will be those who humble themselves before the Lord and learn to tremble at His voice.

This may not sound like much of a method for church growth, but it is God's method of Kingdom growth. In order to work the coming harvest, we are about to experience an unbelievable filling of God's Spirit. In the Church's present condition, the gates are not only somewhat shut to the presence of God but they are also shut to the unchurched who are hungry for the reality of God. Not only are most leaders not entering into the Kingdom, but they stand at the gate and keep out those who would come in (see Mt. 23:13).

The choice before us right now is this: We can either continue to try to operate out of a pharisaical understanding of God and what He is doing, or we can drink the cup the Father hands us. The only way we can glorify the Father is to die to our own wills.

Whose Church Is It Anyway?

The question is, who will be on the throne of the Church? Will it be our intellectual, religious attempts at control, or will it be the voice of the Spirit as we seek first the King? As every Christian leader should know, the Spirit cannot be controlled. If He could be controlled, He would not be the Spirit of the Lord God Jehovah. The pharisaical church, by nature, would rather fight to death than lose control and order. As Proverbs 14:4 implies, God would rather have a mess—which indicates a whole lot of life happening—and then clean up, than have everything nice, polite, and religiously controlled.

God is committed to our growing into peacemaking sons. In His sovereignty, He will use an enemy of the Kingdom, pharisaism, to shake us, break us, and empty us out so He can fill us up. Just as Jesus said in Matthew 10:36, our enemies will be of our own household. No one really knows our weakness like a family member, so it will be those who think they know us best, and who really believe they are doing best, whom the Lord will use to take us through the refiner's fire and bring us under His control.

A Prophetic Invitation to Death

In setting us free of religious strongholds, God is calling us to radical obedience. This obedience leads to death and then, in turn, brings forth eternal life. Jesus knew this exact process when He said:

> *...The hour has come for the Son of Man to be glorified. I tell you the truth, unless a kernel of wheat falls to the ground and dies, it remains only a single seed. But if it dies, it produces many seeds. The man who loves his life will lose it, while the man who hates his life in this world will keep it for eternal life. Whoever serves Me must follow Me...* (John 12:23-26 NIV).

Jesus, out of radical love and full knowledge of what to expect, subjected Himself to the complete will of the Father. As Isaiah prophesied, Jesus was like a sheep silent before its shearers (see Is. 53:7).

Jesus, in Matthew 16, prophetically told Peter He would build His Church on "a rock of revelation"— hearing from the Father. But Jesus also told Peter he would be sifted as wheat (see Lk. 22:31). At that point, Peter was bound and blinded by spiritual pride. Not only was he puffed up by his faith and commitment, but he was so confident in his wisdom that he, under demonic leading, actually rebuked Jesus.

With Peter, unlike Jesus, satan had a legal right to sift him because of his spiritual pride. The Peter who emerged on the beach with Jesus after the resurrection was a broken and humble Peter, a man whom God could trust on the day of Pentecost (see Jn. 21).

Like Peter, many leaders today have a prophetic expectation of God's using them. But before that can be a reality, these leaders must die to self, for God is opposed to the proud. The death process will be so complete we will no longer have any confidence in our abilities and gifts to build the Kingdom.

As Jesus went through the fire of dying to Himself, so must we. Jesus said, "Now My heart is troubled, and what shall I say? 'Father, save Me from this hour'? No, it was for this very reason I came to this hour. Father, glorify Your name!" (Jn. 12:27-28a NIV) We too will end up at a place of hopelessness with only enough faith to say, "Father, into Your hands I commit my being" (see Lk. 24:7).

When we come to the point where we only want the Father's love, wisdom, and sovereignty, we will be where revelation transcends ideals and moves beyond agendas, so that life is extended to the hurt and the broken. Such transcendent revelation is essential because authority comes not from teaching or anointing, but from revelation, which releases authority, which releases power.

The Issue Is Love

Not only is it necessary for us to go through the refiner's fire, but because of sin in the Church, satan has the legal right to demand permission from the Father to test us. I believe that God, in His sovereign timing and wisdom, is at this moment, giving satan permission to begin. Jesus said that in a time of wars and rumors of wars, earthquakes, famines, and droughts, most people's love would grow cold and many would fall away, hate one another, and deliver up one another in betrayal (see Mt. 24).

These calamities, although already in evidence, are about to be greatly multiplied. Christians leaders and other believers who are primarily criticizing, attacking, and condemning other Christians will increase in their vehemence. Leaders will attack leaders— even within specific fellowships—to the point that many churches will fall apart purely from the warfare within. This is already taking place, but it will accelerate.

Sins that the Bible clearly labels as punishable by hell, such as slander, gossip, and lying, will increase in the Church for two basic reasons: First, the Lord wants to move sovereignly; that is, not by our efforts or plans, but by His power and strategy. Pharisaical leaders will be more and more provoked by what they cannot control, understand, or duplicate. As Isaiah says, when God overtly moves, what He does is a "stone of stumbling and...a rock of offence" to the natural, religious mind (Is. 8:14 KJV). First Corinthians 2:10b-14 (NIV) says this:

> *The Spirit searches all things, even the deep things of God ...no one knows the thoughts of God except the Spirit of God. We have not received the spirit of the world but the Spirit who is from God, that we may understand what God has freely given us. This is what we speak, not in words taught us by human wisdom but in words taught by the Spirit, expressing spiritual truths in spiritual words. The man without the Spirit does not accept the things that come from the Spirit of God,*

*for they are foolishness to him, and he cannot under-
stand them, because they are spiritually discerned.*

Second, Pharisaical warfare is more than an attitude.
It is a demonic force that can powerfully deceive us when
we trust mainly in our own understanding. People will
be more and more given over to criticism and pride, preferring the *form* of godliness to the reality of God. The
deception will be so strong that some will be in direct
disobedience to the Bible but will still attempt to bibli-
cally justify their malevolent attacks on other Christians.

Hard-core evidence of the pharisaical spirit is found
when these Christians, especially leaders, are no longer
focused on extending life and resolving issues. Instead,
they judge, condemn, and destroy one another. If Jesus' standards for New Testament prophets were applied to some teaching ministries today, they would be
seen for what they are. Their fruit would speak for itself. When orthodoxy, traditions, and peripheral doctrines are more important than love and acceptance of
brothers, Pharisaism is in control. The problem is, as Jesus said in Matthew 24, love has grown cold.

Spiritual discernment comes from the heart, not the
head. Nevertheless, a great number of Church leaders
operate more from natural wisdom than by spiritual
discernment. This is true because our priorities are
mixed up. We have valued theology and doctrine more
than prayer and worship. In many churches, the concepts of prayer and worship are not truly understood.
They are merely programs to go through.

This practice has brought present Church leadership to the same place as the leadership of Jesus' time: knowing the Scriptures but not recognizing the Messiah. That is, they are ignorant to the point where the Spirit's actions are called demonic.

It may be helpful to note the difference between a "Jezebel spirit" and a pharisaical spirit. The pharisaical person in his own mind, is completely committed to doing the things of God. The problem is, the pharisaical mind confuses the things of God with God Himself. Relationship, compassion, and grace are exchanged for performance, control, and order.

The Jezebel spirit, on the other hand, is as witchcraft in the Body of Christ. Using spiritual gifts, manipulation, and power, the person under a Jezebel influence is fixed on gaining personal power, glory, or money. Both spirits, however, are against the prophetic moving of the Holy Spirit, since the Spirit brings liberty and discernment to God's people to come out of control and/or fear.

Religious Bondage or Spiritual Freedom

Current prophetic activity is exemplified in Second Samuel 6. After David had come into kingship, his heart's desire was to retrieve the Ark of the Covenant, which symbolized the presence of God.

Many of the future Joshuas and Calebs are now coming into strong leadership anointing. And, like David, they are desiring to bring back to the Church the real presence of God as the early Church experienced Him.

As David brought the Ark to the city, the Israelites worshiped the Lord the best they knew how. Irreverently touching the symbolic presence of God, a man called Uzzah (meaning "strength of man") died on the threshing floor.

Uzzah's death is what the Nineties are all about: crossing the threshing floor in reverence and coming into a place of true worship in Spirit and revelatory truth. The Lord is teaching us to "...work out [our] salvation with fear and trembling, for it is God who works in [us] to will and to act according to His good purpose [as opposed to ours]" (Phil. 2:12-13 NIV). David, in frustration and anger over losing his man Uzzah, left the Ark; but he was soon back, provoked to jealousy because the farmer who owned the threshing floor was being blessed by the presence of the Lord.

For those of you who feel like your whole life is one big threshing floor, have hope. God is definitely preparing you for a day of Pentecost in which His glory will move. The key to coming out of the threshing floor successfully is in what David then began to do.

This time, when David came with the Ark, the people were not worshiping merely as tradition dictated. They got radical in demonstrating their love and thanks to the Lord. They went six paces and made a sacrifice to the Lord, after which David danced in the streets with all his might.

It is not a question of dancing or not, but a question of losing ourselves in Him. God is calling us to move beyond the limited understanding of Him we are capable of intellectually, and to begin to treat Him as God. The pharisaical power over the Church is broken when we say, "Father, Your will, not mine!"

In the midst of David's dancing, a pharisaical spirit arose in Michal, David's wife. She felt embarrassed by David's childlike behavior in the streets. She just could not relate to David's being consumed with joy over the presence of the Lord.

Her reaction was a lot like that of Christians today who have little tolerance for prayer and worship. One of the real differences between people who are seeking first the Kingdom of God and people who are focused on churchianity is this: Kingdom people love to worship and pray to the Father, but religious people prefer endless activity.

People who have experienced revelation of the Father, as Ephesians 1:17-18 talks about, become like the woman who used her hair to spread costly perfume on Jesus' feet. Conversely, many consider it a waste, since that time, energy, and money could be spent on more programs. In the spiritual realm, on the other hand, anything not coming out of prayer and worship seems a waste!

Michal, our example of pharisaism, then rebuked David. From that time on she was under a curse. She remained childless, unfruitful. Churches and Christians today who refuse the call of the Spirit to renew their love affair with God will lose their lampstands, which is their witness to the world and their ability to exercise spiritual discernment. Many are already at a place where, in the name of defending theological values, they are becoming anti-biblical in their intent and actions. "Whoever has will be given more...whoever does not have, even what he has will be taken from him" as his heart becomes hardened (Mt. 13:12 NIV).

Lessons From the Threshing Floor

In the face of the present warfare, we have only one recourse: to get on our faces before the Father. The level of spiritual warfare, especially divisive criticism and rejection within the Church, will increase dramatically. If we are not on our knees in love before the Father, we will find ourselves lying on our backs, either in fear before the enemy, or in growing pride and arrogance!

Isaiah 30:15 says, "...In repentance and rest you shall be saved, in quietness and trust is your strength...." Through the power of repentance, on our knees, we can be free to stand before our enemies. Through the power of the Lord's calm, we can be free to storm the gates of hell.

Warfare Strategy Against Pharisaism

When telling the disciples that He was leaving them for a place to which they could not immediately follow, Jesus said, "A new commandment I give to you, that you love one another, even as I have loved you, that you also love one another. By this all men will know that you are My disciples, if you have love for one another" (Jn. 13:3-4).

If we are going to come into the Spirit's movement, we must delve deeper into love and not allow our hearts to be hardened. This is the only way to overcome pharisaical warfare.

Just as God allowed Jesus to be struck down by pharisaical warfare, He will allow many leaders to be struck down and the sheep to be scattered. For some, the warfare of loveless criticism, rejection, and condemnation will come from ones we have shared our cup with. This is why it will be so intense! At the core of the intensity is the issue of love. If we lose our love for God's people, we have lost the battle. If we have lost our love for our brother, we are no longer loving God.

Four principles will arm us against the pharisaical warfare that comes against us through people in our own churches or circles.

First, we need to remember who the enemy is and is not. We do not fight against flesh and blood, but against demonic principalities. So love must rule. This means we pray for our brother who attacks us, and, as much as possible, be peacemakers, that is, sons of God. Remember, people who hurt others usually do so because they themselves are hurting.

Second, we are to walk in humility rather than in self-righteousness. Often, even when an accusation or slander against us is wrong, there may be a grain of truth to it. If we live before the Father in humility, we can be quick to discern the truth, to repent where necessary, and to minister love. In the event the criticism is true, rather than trying to justify ourselves, we need do what Jesus said: "Settle matters quickly with your adversary..." (Mt. 5:25 NIV), so we are not judged. Like my friend Ron Allen says, "The most humble guy wins." Being humble does not mean denying what is true or backing off from the Father's will; rather, it means maintaining love at the cost of personal pride.

Third, we need to let God be our defense. Our strength is in quietness and trust (see Is. 30:15), not in ourselves. When our minds are focused on the Father, His perfect peace can override any situation (see Is. 26:3). Then, in humility and wisdom, we can hear from the Spirit how to pray and what steps to take. (For further reading, see Numbers 12:1-15.)

Fourth, in keeping with First Kings 8:35, we must come before the Lord with a conscious awareness of the afflictions of our hearts. When we approach God in humility, there is a freedom in our lives to allow past bitterness, unforgiveness, or sin to come into the light.

To overcome the coming warfare, we need to appropriate Jesus' payment for sins, so satan can have nothing on us. "In repentance and rest is your salvation" (Is. 30:15 NIV).

This is what the Lord says: "Heaven is My throne, and the earth is My footstool. Where is the house you will build for Me? Where will My resting place be? Has not My hand made all these things, and so they came into being?" declares the Lord. "This is the one I esteem: he who is humble and contrite in spirit, and trembles at My word" (Isaiah 66:1-2 NIV).

Chapter Six

A Jericho Year

Psalm 68:7-10 reads:

O God, when Thou didst go forth before Thy people, when Thou didst march through the wilderness, the earth quaked; the heavens also dropped rain at the presence of God; Sinai itself quaked at the presence of God, the God of Israel. Thou didst shed abroad a plentiful rain, O God; Thou didst confirm Thine inheritance, when it was parched. Thy creatures settled in it; Thou didst provide in Thy goodness for the poor, O God.

Despite the culturally relevant programs and methodology of the contemporary Church, only a sovereign move of God's presence will shake the demonic realm and release the rains of revival on world cultures.

When Adam and Eve decided to "be like God," they exchanged a relationship of childlike dependence on the Father for an adult/adult relationship where they could be in control of their lives. Part of the curse they stepped into when exiting the garden was to face responsibility for their own needs. They had to work by the sweat of their brow in order to survive.

In like manner, it is only by the sweat of Jesus' blood, in His childlike obedience to the Father in the second garden, that man can leave the slavery of performance and come again into a childlike dependence on the Father's power and provision. As Paul said, "For you did not receive a spirit that makes you a slave again to fear, but you received the spirit of sonship. And by Him we cry 'Abba Father' " (Rom. 8:15 NIV).

As a consequence of the fall, man has had a major conflict between trustingly obeying God and doing things from his own wisdom and strength. As Isaiah said, "In repentance and rest is your salvation, in quietness and trust is your strength, but you would have none of it" (Is. 30:15b NIV).

Frequently there is great conflict in letting God be God in our churches, where religious spirits and people sometimes prefer religious activity to spiritual worship.

Primarily, religious activity gets in the way of the Holy Spirit's movement; this is the "Martha syndrome." Man, oftentimes with good intentions, falls into the trap of doing busywork for God rather than listening and acting out of obedience. We must not forget, however, that to obey is always better than just giving God our religious sacrifices (see 1 Sam. 15:22). He does not need them anyway.

Laying our busyness aside, we must respond to the Holy Spirit. Over the past few years, as many leaders are aware, the Holy Spirit has been releasing within the Body of Christ two heart cries, for prayer and for worship.

Both are completely central to the last days' Church. By these main disciplines, we experience communication with the Father and know His presence and specific will. They are the keys to intimacy with God that will allow the contemporary Church to enter into what the Father is doing.

If one single verse captures the Spirit's message to the present Church, it is Psalm 46:10 (NIV): "Be still, and know that I am God; I will be exalted among the nations, I will be exalted in the earth." Most of the time, when God is overtly on the move, He deliberately operates in seemingly childish and offensive ways. This is because the Kingdom is being built on a rock of revelation that is a "stone of stumbling and a rock of offense" to religious paradigms (1 Pet. 2:8).

At the end of 1992, I prayed about the year to come. I heard the Lord say that it was to be a Jericho year, that is, a year of breakthrough in radical worship. For many churches that is a year. The word *radical* in Latin is the word *roots*, meaning "core beginnings." In essence, the Lord was calling the Church back to its roots: a radical first love of Jesus. The call was to desire foremost to worship and obey Him, instead of focusing on religiously fulfilling the status quo.

This was the preparation Israel underwent prior to marching on Jericho. The Israelites' worship really began years before when they sent out spies (see Num. 23). Among the 12 tribes, only Joshua and Caleb had faith that God could give them victory over the giants in the land.

As previously stated, many Joshuas and Calebs are being released now to lead a more obedient generation of people. The Church renewal of the Sixties and Seventies was powerful, but many of that renewal movement still lived without really seeking first the King's will for their lives. It will be the children of the renewal generation who will, metaphorically speaking, take the Church across the Jordan.

The radical call on the next generation is a stumbling block for the older generation as it looks at all the current cultural rebellion. But the inverse of what Jesus said in Luke 7:47b is, "Those who are forgiven much, love much."

A Time of Circumcision

Upon crossing the Jordan, the Israelites immediately purified themselves by circumcising the men. Even though they were of a generation raised in freedom, the outward sign of Egypt—slavery—was still on them and they needed to be cleansed from this.

For the last few years, many Christians have been going through a similar process of spiritual circumcision. Our circumcision is not of the flesh, as was the Israelites', but of the heart. Though all Christians are "saved" by the blood of the Lamb and are going to Heaven, much of the Church today is still bound by attitudes and values of the world, which makes it difficult for us to serve God freely. As Jesus said, "No one can serve two masters..." (Mt. 6:24 NIV).

In this period of restoration, the Lord, by grace, has initially ordained a time for us to respond to His heart. This is a period of grace on top of grace, as it were, in which we can choose to fall on the rock and be broken, as opposed to later on when the rock will fall on us if we are not broken and humble us before God and man (see Mt. 21:44).

As time elapses (I see about a 12- to 15-year period, which is about the same foundational period the first church in Jerusalem experienced), judgment will visibly increase on those of God's household who ignore the voice of the Spirit. As God increasingly allows satan to sift the Church, anointing and God's provision will lift, and protection against the enemy will lessen. Those who resist the grace of the voice of the Spirit and refuse to repent, God the Father will discipline in love.

It is always easier to fall on the rock instead of having it fall on you. Thus those churches that respond and return to their first love, as many did in 1993, will enjoy breakthroughs in the area of evangelism. They will see some of the enemy's walls come down.

The plan for overthrowing Jericho was not a slick strategy, but was actually a plan that made no sense to the natural mind. The power was not in the plan, but in the obedience of following what God told Joshua to do. And that began as Joshua received a fresh revelation of the Lord, as told in Joshua 5:13-15. Before he could go out against Jericho, it was completely necessary for Joshua to get this deeper revelation of God. His response as he met with the "Captain of the host of the

Lord" was to fall down on his face in worship and ask the Lord to speak to Him.

As He did with Joshua, the Lord now stands between His people and the fortressed walls of the cities around us. And, as in Joshua 5, the Lord is holding a sword in His hand; He is ready for battle. This sword, of course, is the sword of the Spirit, which consists of words God speaks to His people.

Like the end-time church of Laodicea in Revelation 3, the question is, who has the ears to hear what the Spirit is saying to the Church? The key message for the end-time Church is, get hot before we are spit out of the mouth of the Lord. When it comes to intimacy with God, we will either go forward or fall behind.

For many leaders, even what they have experienced in revelation and discernment will be taken away if they do not respond to God's call to prayer and worship. The first six days of the Israelites' silent marching around Jericho with the Ark symbolized the first six months of 1993. It was a time of listening to the Lord and allowing Him to give new vision, of going with His presence outside the four walls of the Church. This was followed in midsummer by a fresh freedom to take the presence of the Lord public, through praise and worship. This season, sovereignly ordained by the Lord, was a time for God's people to venture beyond the church's walls and, with the high praise of God on our lips as swords, go forth against the walled fortresses of our cultures.

Proclamation Worship

Since then, in addition to the "March for Jesus" in which many Christians participate annually, God continues to give unique strategies to different churches about new ways of going forth and proclaiming His glory. Much of this is public ministry, like good works and aid to the poor, but the heart of it centers around worship.

There are many different types of worship, such as intimate worship, singing the Lord's promises, rejoicing in His love, etc. What some call "warfare worship" has been popular in some churches for quite awhile. Proclamation worship, by definition, is a "going forth with a shout" right into the face of the adversaries in the public arena, and proclaiming God's sovereignty and glory over all the earth.

One classic biblical example that demonstrates the relationship between worship, God's presence, and the gospel's growth is found in Acts 16, when Paul and Silas were locked up in Philippi. Despite their chains, Paul and Silas engaged in proclamation worship, freely singing praise to God before the other inmates—right in the enemy's camp, so to speak. God responded to their worship with a mighty shaking of the prison. Prisoners were set free and many came to accept Jesus. From this we see that when people worship, God shows up, and the Kingdom grows.

Of course, worship is not a magic formula for protection. In Paul and Silas' case, their worship invited attack from the enemy. Before their arrest, they had been on their way to "the place of prayer." En route, they were accosted by a slave girl with a spirit of divination. After this girl hounded them for several days, Paul rebuked the spirit, which then left the girl. Consequently, the girl was no longer able to tell fortunes, and her owners lost revenue. In anger, they had Paul and Silas arrested. This parallels our times; the demonic realm is increasingly overt, and the real prince in control over the demonic is the spirit of mammon, or money, at least in our Western culture.

There is an important lesson for us here. Many think that everything will get better outwardly if they just pray more. On the contrary, the more we pray, the more the demonic realm tries to prevent us from praying. Demonic hindrances will increase, and persecution will increase. God allows this because He wants us to completely depend on Him.

The good news for us, however, is that often as outward situations worsen, we find an increase in the Lord's anointing on our lives. We come to the place of the disciples in the boat: surrounded by a terrible storm but with the Holy Spirit drawing near. The question is, who will stay in the boat of Matthew 14:22, clinging to a false sense of security in the system, and who will say, "Lord, can we walk with You on the water?" Only one of the disciples dared to get out of the boat.

When we look at the history of the Lord with Israel, we see quite often that only the tribe of Judah was spared the judgments on the whole nation. When Israel would pray about which tribe should go first into battle, the Lord would say, "Judah shall go first" (Judg. 20:18;1:2). It is the Lord's desire that we be like Judah.

The word *Judah* comes from the Hebrew root *yadah*. This word has two basic meanings: first, to confess who God is—the absolute King of all that exists, and the all-powerful God of great glory who is the very definition of love. Second, it means to confess our shortcomings in comparison with our God, for He is a God of complete holiness. Emulating Judah, those who lead the attack against the "walled fortresses" of our cultures will be those who learn to worship in the presence of the Spirit of God, in the truth of who He is, and in the reality of who we are in His light.

Spiritual pride can be a hindrance to this type of worship. Indeed, spiritual pride is the area of imagined self-sufficiency that most upsets to the Lord. From satan's and Adam's falls to the stance of many Church leaders today, there is a posture of imagined strength, a complete self-confidence in our own gifts and abilities. With the utmost presumption, we may feel capable of performing God's work by speaking it into existence without even seeking Him.

Isaiah 66:12 makes clear that it is not those who think they can do it, but those who are broken before God, who will build the Lord's house. Psalm 127:1 says that unless He, the Lord, is the builder, we labor in vain.

Like Paul and Silas, much of the Church is headed toward becoming a house of prayer. But in order for us to be a people upon whom the Lord can look, we need to be humble and broken before Him. The result will be that even when our plans and strategies seem to be waylaid, we will learn to turn our failures and prisons into places of prayer and worship. We will begin to trust that even in worst-case scenarios, God can and will glorify Himself. The battle is, in fact, the Lord's.

The Eleventh-Hour Shaking

Back in Philippi, Paul and Silas, after being arrested, were beaten and locked up, and their feet were put in stocks. Often in the Bible, feet symbolize our ability to go forward with the gospel. Isaiah 52:7 reads, "How lovely on the mountains are the feet of him who brings good news, who announces peace and brings good news of happiness, who announces salvation..." In the New Testament, Paul tells the Ephesian saints to "shod your feet with the preparation of the gospel of peace" (Eph. 6:15). In order for our feet to leave the prisons of our safe, comfortable altars of orthodoxy and move out with the gospel of peace, we definitely need a bigger revelation of God, His sovereignty, and especially His perfect love that casts out fear.

"...about midnight Paul and Silas were praying and singing hymns of praise to God, and the prisoners were listening to them" (Acts 16:25). As we enter into perhaps the "eleventh hour" of the Church age, God is doing a new thing with prayer and worship—not that what He is doing is new in Scripture, but the depth of it is new to the Body of Christ today.

The end-time Church will be a house of prayer. We will become a people who, not only in our theology but in our lives, worship the Father in Spirit and in truth. As with Joshua before the battle of Jericho, we need a greater personal revelation of God's love and power, one that will put us on our faces before God in a listening mode so that we might learn to work out our salvation with fear and trembling (see Phil. 2:12).

Again, as Paul and Silas were worshiping, the Lord shook the house down to its foundation, the doors were thrown open, and the chains were unfastened. The final outcome was so powerful that even the jailer and his whole family came to the Lord. This is the outpouring of the Spirit that will meet with the Church as we learn to worship the Father in Spirit and in truth.

What the Church and the world desperately need today is a sovereign shaking by God's presence. We do not need to be *raptured* so much as we need to be *recaptured* by *the truth* that Jesus Christ is Lord of everything, even in the dirty now-and-now, not just in the sweet by-and-by. The role of the Church is to be the scriptural people the Bible tells us to be: people of prayer and worship, people who obey every word that proceeds from the mouth of God.

The bottom line is that to obey is better than to make religious sacrifices. In fact, the real sacrifice the Lord desires is for us to become broken and humble before His throne, a people who delight in doing the Father's will. As with the people of Jesus' time, we desperately need a radical, root-level revelation of God to turn over the tables in the temple of our hearts. Because we are coming into a unique period in history, it is time for us to be still and to listen. It will be a time when God touches world cultures and populations to a deeper extent than the world has ever experienced. So great will be His touch that even many of the enemies of God's people will be saved, just like with the jailer of Paul and Silas.

I know that You can do all things; no plan of Yours can be thwarted. ...Surely I spoke of things I did not understand, things too wonderful for me to know. You said, "Listen now, and I will speak: I will question you, and you shall answer Me." My ears had heard of You but now my eyes have seen You. Therefore I despise myself and repent in dust and ashes (Job 42:2-6 NIV).

A Postscript

As a two-year postscript to the spring letter that comprised this chapter, I would like to relate the following story that happened at Foothills Christian Fellowship in El Cajon, California (my home-away-from-home church). It took place during the spring of 1994, when the church ran renewal meetings, Toronto style, for seven consecutive weeks.

In the midst of the renewal and the excitement around the outpouring of the Holy Spirit, one of the girls from the church invited her unsaved teenage friend who was suffering from anorexia. She was profoundly touched by the Holy Spirit that night and promptly surrendered her life to Jesus. Her parents, having come out of cult involvement, were furious upon hearing of her experience and forbade her to attend any more meetings. But over the next few days, the father noticed the absence of anger and rebellion in their daughter and saw so profound a change in her personality and behavior that they agreed to accompany her to the Sunday morning service. After the service, they were invited to one of the church family's home for lunch. They then went back to the church for the evening service, where the father was prayed for and gave his life to Jesus. Within a few days at another renewal meeting, he was powerfully touched by the Holy Spirit. Over a period of the following few weeks, not only the mother, but a teenage son and a 12-year-old son all gave their lives to Jesus. The parents' marriage has been turned around, and the family as a whole is now living for Jesus and is highly involved in the life of the church.

In this chapter, as I considered the incident of Paul and Silas worshiping God while firmly locked up in jail, I was reminded of this story from El Cajon. Metaphorically speaking, in the renewal move of the last two years, the outpouring of the Holy Spirit has been shaking the Church just as God shook the jail in Philippi. God shook this church by the power of His presence, and a small part of the fruit was that an entire family came to Jesus and entered into abundant life. As Haggai prophesied, "This is what the Lord Almighty says: 'In a little while I will once more shake the heavens and the earth, the sea and the dry land. I will shake all nations, and the desired of all nations will come, and I will fill this house with glory,' says the Lord Almighty" (Hag. 2:6-7 NIV).

Lord, let everything that can be shaken be shaken so that Your glory reigns!

Chapter Seven

Understanding the Role of Prophetic Ministries Today

In Ezekiel 1 and Revelation 4, two different prophets describe similar visions of four beings representing worship and the will of God. One being had the face of a lion, the second an eagle, the third an ox, and the fourth was like a man. Among other things, the four beings depict the fourfold ministerial offices Paul mentions in Ephesians, chapter 4.

The ox is symbolic of the pastor/teacher, the steady worker whose success is measured not in bursts of power or glory, but in the day-in-day-out, steady, and patient plodding of a shepherd. The man portrays the evangelist, the office that best relates the truths of God to those who do not know Him. The lion represents the apostle, the power and authority in the jungle, so to speak, of one sent to release the King's order. (It is no mistake that many monarchies use the lion in their crests or emblems.) Finally, the eagle figures the prophet, one who is slightly set apart, who soars in the highest places, but who also has the best vision to see what is happening a long way off.

As I said in the first chapter, we are entering the times Joel spoke of, when the Lord is touching all humanity and is wanting His people to have eyes to see and ears to hear.

In the midst of God's raising up prophetic ministries in a new way, it is important to understand not only the purpose of these ministries but also their limitations.

You Shall All Know the Lord

Understanding the purpose and limitations of the prophetic is essential if the Church wishes to stabilize the typical pendulum reaction to prophecy—from Pharisaic fear to quick-fix thinking. Five basic but important distinctions between Old and New Testament prophetic ministries aid our understanding.

First is authority. The prophets in the Old Testament had tremendous authority, in varying degrees, because they were the only ones who could hear from the Lord on a regular basis. In contrast, today all Christians have anointing from the Holy Spirit to know God and to be led in a very personal Father/child relationship.

So the basic distinction between the old and new covenant has incredible ramifications regarding New Testament prophetic ministry. In Jeremiah 31:33-34 (NIV) the Lord declares, "...I will put My law in their minds and write it on their hearts. I will be their God, and they will be My people. No longer will a man teach his neighbor, or a man his brother, saying, 'Know the Lord,' because they will all know Me, from the least of them to the greatest...." First John 2:27 (NIV) in a similar vein says, "...the anointing you received from Him remains in you, and you do not need anyone to teach you. But as His anointing teaches you about all things and as that anointing is real, not counterfeit...."

The most crucial truth of the gospel is not only that a legal payment has been paid but that now we might also know God on a highly personal basis. Jesus did not come merely to give us free fire insurance; He came to restore man to a relationship of intimacy with God.

Up to the time of the resurrection, only a few select individuals actually had the Spirit of God in their lives. Those who received this anointing were prophets, judges, some kings, and a few other people. And that anointing was not what we call being "born again." The Spirit on them was often an anointing, or a capacity, to do the Lord's will. This was why, when confronted by Nathan the prophet for sinning with Bathsheba, David so ardently sought to retain the Spirit's anointing (see David's prayer in Psalm 51).

Our anointing and intimacy with God does not take away the need for pastors, leaders, and teachers; nonetheless, as individuals, our lives are to be directed by God and not man. One of the very basic scriptural examples of this principle is found in Second Corinthians 9:7 (NIV), "Each man should give what he has decided in his heart to give, not reluctantly or under compulsion, for God loves a cheerful giver." Many churches that abuse authority manipulate people concerning money. But the basic principle of the new covenant is that we are to be led by the Spirit as opposed to being controlled by man.

One classic biblical example of this is seen in Acts 21, when the respected prophet Agabus came to Paul with a prophetic warning of what would happen to him if he went to Jerusalem. The people who heard that prophecy attempted to persuade Paul to heed the prophecy and not go. But Paul reserved the right to be directed by the inner voice of God in his life. This did not subtract from the authenticity of Agabus' ministry; indeed, his word was fulfilled, but it meant Paul had to process that word through the grid of his own wisdom, experience, faith, and personal leading of the Holy Spirit.

First Corinthians 14:3 (NIV) says that prophecy is for the purpose of "strengthening, encouragement and comfort." Nowhere in the New Testament does it say anything about prophecies controlling, manipulating, or condemning anyone. "Directional" prophecies, either personal or corporate, must be worked through the framework of God's children as they are led by the Spirit as individuals (see Rom. 8:14).

Obviously, leaders are called to lead, preach, teach, and sometimes rebuke. But when it comes to individual choice as to how, when, and where to serve God, we must walk in the priesthood that Jesus died to give us.

Contemporary Prophecy Versus "Thus Sayeth the Lord"

The second difference between prophecy then and now also has to do with differences of delegated authority between *logos* and *rhema*. Today, because the Bible is complete, all prophecy will be *rhema*, as opposed to *logos*. The general distinction between *logos* and *rhema* is that the inspired it was intended by God to affect His people not just one time, but throughout the ages, eventually being canonized into what we call the Bible.

Rhema is also inspired by the Holy Spirit, but it is meant for only a specific person or group, a specific situation, and a specific time. In other words, the difference between *logos* and *rhema* is the difference between general and specific truth.

Rhema not meant to be canonized as the *logos* was also around in Old Testament times. Many Bible teachers today say that the gift of prophecy does not exist now because the Bible is complete. This argument overlooks the full use of prophecy in the Bible. There were often groups of prophets, such as the "sons of the prophets" in Samuel, that obviously prophesied, but their words were not meant to be canonized. Acts 11:27 and 13:1 talks about prophets, including Agabus, but we do not have any major messages from them—as we do from Samuel, Isaiah, or Jeremiah—that were intended as instruction for our lives.

Again, the question is not whether God actually speaks today, for He most certainly does. The point is,

God does not delegate authority to prophecies or to prophetic ministries in the same way as in Old Testament times.

In a seminar entitled "Developing the Prophetic Church: Learning to Converse with the Father," I encourage people not to preface prophetic words with "Thus sayeth the Lord." I believe that phrase implies a measure of authority the Holy Spirit does not intend. When a word of *rhema* is prayed, it should be processed through the individual's own priesthood rather than to be obeyed in blind obedience.

I sometimes refer to personal prophecy concerning future direction and goals as a "diving board into a pool of prayer." As an individual seeks the Lord for confirmation, he or she is likely open to hearing things from the Lord that otherwise might not be heard. Often, what the Lord in His goodness has prepared for our futures is either too good or too radically different for us to imagine. At this point, an outside word can open us to new perspectives.

As First Corinthians 2:9 (NIV) says, "...No eye has seen, no ear has heard, no mind has conceived what God has prepared for those who love Him."

Mercy and Compassion Versus Wrath and Judgment

Another key difference in correctly handling prophecy today is understanding that through Christ judgment has been paid. Jesus did not come to destroy, but to bring abundant life. Often "wanna-be" prophets and individuals who actually do have prophetic gifting use as their role models prophets like Elijah and Jeremiah. The problem with this is that such latter-day prophets fail to get the whole picture of their role model's hearts.

The classic example is when James and John, the "sons of thunder," wanted to call down fire from heaven to destroy a Samaritan village. Their model was Elijah when he called down fire from heaven to destroy two companies of soldiers. In righteous wrath and indignation on behalf of Jesus, James and John wanted the people destroyed. Jesus replied to them, "...You do not know what kind of spirit you are of; for the Son of Man did not come to destroy men's lives, but to save them..." (Lk. 9:55-56).

The point is clear: The Holy Spirit does not gift people in order to destroy. Some would say that the Lord's judgment of Ananias and Sapphira in Acts 5 disproves this, but there is no clear proof that Peter confronted them in front of the entire congregation. That the young men were outside the door when Peter spoke to Sapphira suggests it was a small gathering. In any event, the lying to the Holy Spirit was serious enough in that situation that God did not allow any future chance of repentance, at least in this dimension.

Many times I hear of prophetic ministries that, in public, rebuke, condemn, and speak out hidden sins. It is as if the prophetic office were a quick-fix operation for ailing churches. It is not enough to be able to see the truth, however, because satan himself is constantly seeing our sins and accusing us before the throne of God. On the contrary, Isaiah 42:3 uses two phrases to describe a struggling believer, saying that Jesus would not "break a bent reed" or blow out a "flickering wick."

For many who have come to Christ, these two phrases aptly identify them. To become whole is not a quick fix; it is learning to work out their salvation in fear and trembling, with much love, acceptance, and wisdom applied as part of the healing process.

When truth comes without love, the result is usually death and destruction. It was the Pharisees who, with no love or compassion, dragged the woman caught in adultery in front of Jesus and the crowd (see Mt. 8:3). Jesus, in speaking to her, said He did not condemn her.

Many times while I have been ministering, the Lord has pointed out to me sins and hypocrisy about people, but there are ways of dealing rebukes and warnings without destroying a person. It is satan who brings condemnation to destroy. It is the Spirit of God who convicts, bringing encouragement unto repentance. As Psalm 85:10 says, "Lovingkindness and truth have met together; righteousness and peace have kissed each other."

Yes, God gives prophetic insight into hidden sins, but a prophet who only sees the truth but does not know the Father's heart can also be a false prophet because he is not truly representing the character of God.

God's Authority Is Both Inherent and Delegated

Another problematic area for many churches and especially leaders is prophetic people who do not understand delegated authority. These are the wanna-be's who cloud themselves in cloaks of mysticism. They are above accountability to any pastor or church leader on the premise that "they are hearing from God," and everyone needs to submit to their revelation. Implicit in their message is their special "pipe line" to God that renders them spiritually superior to basic Bible principles.

The point here is the difference between God's inherent authority and His delegated authority. In Old Testament times, prophets like Samuel and Elijah occasionally had more authority even than kings. But, as discussed earlier, there is a radical difference between God's delegated authority to prophets then and now.

Possibly the only parallel now to a prophet like Elijah would be the office of apostle. Even there, biblical guidelines for relationship and accountability still apply. If people are actually walking with God, they will have proper regard not only for what God is calling them to do but also in respecting God's anointing and authority in others.

Obviously, Jesus had no sin to repent of. Yet when He came to John the Baptist, as told in Luke 3, He submitted to John's prophetic call to be baptized. Jesus respected the authority the Father had given John.

The principle of accountability and fellowship is firmly established in the New Testament. Hebrews

13:17 (NIV) reads, "Obey your leaders and submit to their authority. They keep watch over you as men who must give an account. Obey them so that their work will be a joy, not a burden, for that would be of no advantage to you."

Many pseudo-prophets are in real sin. They lead a lifestyle of being belligerent and forceful in trying to usurp a pastor's or elder's authority. Part of the problem is that God often gifts some individuals in a fellowship to a greater degree of prophetic anointing than some of the leaders.

The situation can grow into a problem if one or two things are happening: (1) the leaders are insecure and are unable to receive questions or encouragement from the body; (2) those prophetically gifted are not honoring the authority God has given their leaders. James 3:17 (NIV) says, "...wisdom that comes from heaven is first of all pure; then peace-loving, considerate, submissive, full of mercy and good fruit, impartial and sincere." He contrasts this with earthly wisdom, which stems from envy and selfish ambition.

Much of the time, self-styled "prophets" cause headaches and division for leaders. These prophets perhaps see the truth in part, but they operate out of false ambition for power and control. The New American Standard translation of James 3:17 says that wisdom from above is " reasonable," meaning that it can be discussed and prayed through, as opposed to being manipulative and controlling.

Two of the main characteristics I look for in prophets, even more than accuracy, is humility of character and scriptural relationships with leaders in the Body of Christ.

Accuracy and the Learning Curve

One main argument against prophetic gifting today is the claim no one nowadays is absolutely perfect in all prophecies. My primary objection to this line of reason is that, in looking at the New Testament, I am not even sure the point is valid theologically. Jesus never said that we would know a prophet by how accurate his prophecies are; rather, a prophet can be tested by the fruit of his ministries (see Mt. 7:15-16).

In First Corinthians Paul says, "Two or three prophets should speak, and the others should weigh carefully what is said" (1 Cor. 14:29 NIV). He does not say let two or three wanna-be's prophesy, but let two or three prophets prophesy. The inference is clear: There were people in the Church at that time who definitely had the gift of prophecy, but their words needed to be judged.

Basically, a prophetic word can come from one of three sources: (1) from the Holy Spirit; (2) from one's own imagination; or (3) from the spiritual realm other than the Holy Spirit.

For the average person to take risks and grow in knowing the difference between his own mind and the spiritual realm, it probably takes years, if not a lifetime. I am not implying that God cannot speak clearly, but it may take a listening prophet years to unlearn the motives and confusion of the world. Until that time, it can be easy for the "eyes and ears of our hearts" to taint or filter what we hear and see. With the gift of prophecy, like most of life, there is going to be a learning curve that will involve mistakes.

Several factors go into making up a checklist for judging a prophecy: (1) Is it scriptural in theme? (2) Does it bring peace, even though it may call for a radical shift in focus? (3) Do two or more mature people bear witness with it? (4) Are people encouraged to draw closer to the Lord, or is it just comprised of pseudo-spiritual words?

The main thing I look for in a prophetic ministry is long-term fruit. Are people being encouraged to seek after the Lord? Are people going deeper into prayer, holiness, and obedience to the Lord? Is life coming forth as a result of the ministry? Jesus, in talking about knowing the Father's will, said to ask the Father for food (see Lk. 11:11-13). We can trust Him not to give us a snake (symbolic for demonic deception).

Jesus also promised us that the Holy Spirit would lead us and guide us into all truth (see Jn. 16:13). Still, just like every other area of life, we enter in as beginners and we learn to walk as children. Sometimes this involves making mistakes. The key is the motivation of our hearts. If we are honestly attempting to serve God, by His grace we will bear fruit in the long run because He does want His children to be led by His Spirit (see Rom. 8:14).

Comfort, Strength, and Encouragement

Last, I see a change in priorities reflecting changes in the covenants and the outpouring of the Holy Spirit. I believe the main function of a prophetic ministry should be to reproduce itself. There is a parallel here with the office of evangelist. What an evangelist is to the unchurched, the prophet should be to the Church. Evangelists who are current with the Holy Spirit will also put a strong emphasis on training ordinary Christians in evangelism. Likewise, prophetic ministries should also teach and train the Body of Christ in the art of intimacy with God.

On a final note, the true function of a prophet is still the same as it was in the time of Samuel: to encourage God's people to draw closer to the heart of the Lord. In fact, the true prophet is one who is used by God to point out, with love and charity, the heart and throne of God. The difference today is that prophets and prophecy are given to encourage and build up individuals in their own priesthood that we might truly be a nation of priests.

I, the Lord, have called you in righteousness; I will take hold of your hand. I will keep you and will make you to be a covenant for the people and a light for the Gentiles, to open eyes that are blind, to free captives from prison and to release from the dungeon those who sit in darkness. I am the Lord; that is My name! I will not give My glory to another or My praise to idols. See, the former things have taken place, and new things I declare; before they spring into being I announce them to you (Isaiah 42:6-9 NIV).

The revelation of Jesus Christ, which God gave Him to show His servants... (Revelation 1:1 NIV).

Chapter Eight

The Year of the Lion

Everyone who has surrendered his or her life to the Lord Jesus has experienced a revelation of the Lamb of God. Much of the Church, seemingly, has not really experienced a revelation of Jesus' other side—that is the Lion of the tribe of Judah.

For many Christians, much of the battle between "salvation" Christianity (where the focus is on being saved) and "lordship" Christianity (where the focus is on being a disciple) has to do with lack of revelation. A lack of revelation stems from a lack of basic intimacy with God. This results in partial heart knowledge, or spiritual knowledge, of who Christ is. It follows, then, that ministry suffers, for it is from the heart rather than the head that life and real ministry flow. Jesus said, "The good man brings good things out of the good stored up in his heart..." (Lk. 6:45 NIV).

At the close of each year, I typically spend the last few weeks seeking the Lord's overriding theme for my messages in the coming year. In December of 1993, without receiving full insight, the Lord drew my focus to

Amos 3:8, which says, "The lion has roared! Who will fear? The Lord God has spoken! Who can but prophesy?"

As 1994 unfolded—with the Holy Spirit's outpouring in Toronto and in many other areas in the Western world, especially North America and England—the Lord clarified His message. Since January of that year, thousands of Christians from all over the globe have come to the Airport Vineyard Christian Fellowship in Toronto, where they have been touched significantly by the Holy Spirit.

A conservative estimate is that somewhere in excess of 100,000 people—many of whom have come from other countries and even other continents—have come to Toronto from January 1994 to January 1995 and encountered the Lord in a life-changing way. More than 10,000 pastors from all over North America, Europe, and other continents have come and experienced both refreshment and new impartations of gifts and power from the Lord (see Acts 3:19).

It would be incorrect to label this phenomenon as "revival," because true revival involves great numbers of first-time conversions. Nevertheless, we can confidently say that the current move of the Holy Spirit is part of His preparation for major revival in the Church.

The present outpouring is affecting the Church in two primary ways. First, those who are weary are being refreshed. Second, those who are in varying stages of a "prodigal" condition are coming home to a party the Father is throwing.

With the same time frame as the Toronto outpouring, countless similar outbreaks of the Holy Spirit are occurring in churches and multi-church gatherings across North America. It seems, however, that Toronto, is one of the major "wellsprings."

This is partial fulfillment of a four-page, two-part prophecy, I received from the Lord in May 1992 and June 1993, concerning Toronto. Very simply, the vision was of living waters like Niagara Falls coming over the city and flowing like a mighty river eastward across Canada and then to the nations. Because of what God is doing, it behooves us to discover His goal and what He wants to release to His people this year.

A Prophetic Renewal of Worship

First Kings 13 illustrates what the Lord is doing. It describes a basic tale of conflict between the Holy Spirit and Pharisaism, wrongful motives, and tradition. It begins with a prophet coming to Bethel ("house of the Lord" in Hebrew) from Judah. The word *Judah* means "praise," but its connotations go even deeper. First, one confesses God's attributes; second, in the light or revelation of who God truly is, one confesses his or her shortcomings and weaknesses.

A major part of the prophetic restoration God has for His people today is a renewal of true worship. As our worship is renewed, we learn to wait on His Spirit and respond to Him instead of merely going through the motions. We learn by revelation that God is the great I Am, and we are the great "we're not"!

One element of the Toronto meetings—and of meetings in other cities as well—that speaks to me is not the power, laughter, or the manifestations, but the worship. People's hunger for God, coming together night after night and sometimes worshiping for an hour or more is, I believe, a true sign of the renewal God wants to bring to His Bride—a return to our first love.

Worship, along with prayer, is not only the battleground in the Nineties, but it is the meeting place from which God will send His people out to do battle. Judges 1:2 (NIV) reads, "The Lord answered, 'Judah is to go; I have given the land into their hands.' " Judges 20:18 (NIV) similarly says, "The Israelites went up to Bethel and inquired of God. They said, 'Who of us shall go first to fight against the Benjamites?' The Lord replied, 'Judah shall go first.' "

The second passage concerns Israel's bringing restoration to the Hebrew people. In the same way today, God wants to release His heart and passion into His people so that we are freed of the complacency, fear, and unbelief within ourselves and we can go after the enemy without.

In First Kings 13, the king who resisted a prophetic message is an exact picture of many leaders today who have made an idol out of order and control, and who insist their traditions and methods in ministry are the only way. In such churches, concern for healing people and setting them free can be secondary to maintaining the program. Too many leaders are far more concerned with protecting *their* empire instead of seeking the Kingdom of God and being right with Him.

As the prophet rebuked the false worship, the king stretched out his hand and gave orders to seize him. But as he did so, his arm and hand completely withered to the point that he was unable to withdraw it.

This is a crucial lesson leaders must learn. The Holy Spirit can be grieved. In this time when He is pouring out revelation of the Father's heart and glory, judgment will be released if leaders respond in an attitude of criticism, trying to keep a hold on their own empires and traditions. Attitudes and the characteristics of pharisaism, such as critical hearts, lack of mercy, and legalism, will begin to overwhelmingly dominate them. In short, God will partially give them over to one of the chief sins a Christian can commit: grieving the Holy Spirit.

One thing God hates, according to Proverbs 6:19 (NIV), is "...a man who stirs up dissension among brothers." In the "true fast" of Isaiah 58, God warns us to put away the pointing of the finger. Like the king in the story, many leaders who pharisaically attack the Spirit's work will end up increasingly devoid of love and humility.

As Paul states in Second Corinthians 3:6 (NIV), we are to be ministers "...not of the letter but of the Spirit; for the letter kills, but the Spirit gives life." Just as the king's condition was evident to all in First Kings 13, if God, from a grieved heart, removes part of His grace from some ministries, those leaders' true motives will be exposed. As the old fable goes, everyone will know that the "king is naked."

Malachi 3:18 (NIV) reads, "And you will again see the distinction ...between those who serve God and those who do not." In First Kings, the king quickly repented, the prophet prayed for him, and the king was healed. The king then offered the prophet a reward, but the prophet replied that the Lord had told him to go home without even eating or drinking, and to return by a different route. As Elisha once asked his servant, "Is this the time to take money, or to accept clothes, olive groves, vineyards, flocks, herds, or menservants and maidservants?" (2 Kings 5:26b NIV)

This is a lesson for those who would respond today. We must not let our hearts become filled with pride and attitudes of elitism, but we must receive God's heart for the whole Body of Christ.

An Hour Has Come

The Book of John presents a picture of the discipleship times we are in. Jesus said, in John 12:23, that the hour had come for the Son of Man to be glorified. He then began to speak of dying to one's self and of being like seed that is buried in the ground but then bears fruit. He ended by stating that He was contemplating the cost the Father was calling Him to make. John 12:27 (NIV) quotes Jesus as saying, "My heart is troubled."

There are two key points here for us today. One, we are, so to speak, in the eleventh hour of history. This is a time when, as the prophet Joel stated, the Spirit of God will touch all mankind (see Joel 2:28). But to enter into Jesus' sort of discipleship, we must die to our own agendas and goals.

Two, if Jesus' soul was troubled by the price tag He would have to pay to be obedient to the Father, it will certainly be a troubling cost that you and I will need to pay. Nonetheless, this is what God is looking for at a time when He is pursuing the nations: people who are so radically in love with Him they are willing to die for Him.

Continuing the account in First Kings 13, as the prophet journeyed home, he was greeted by an older prophet who told him it was okay with God if he came home with him and ate a meal. So the younger prophet went with the elder. But even as they were at the table, the older prophet, by the Spirit of the Lord, rebuked the younger for failing to carry out the whole word of the Lord.

The younger prophet went on his way, but a lion came out of the wilderness and killed him. On hearing this, the older prophet went after him and found him dead in the road. Interestingly, the dead man had been neither eaten nor mauled by the lion. Moreover, sitting by the body was both the lion and the prophet's unafraid donkey. Obviously, this was no ordinary lion; this is a picture of the Lion of the tribe of Judah.

This may sound like a harsh Old Testament story to Christians today, but I believe this vividly depicts God's jealousy over those to whom He gives revelation of Himself (see Jas. 4:5).

We are in a major time of God's Spirit moving on the nations. In the coming years, God will radically call His people to abandon themselves to seeking Him and His will. He will call many into missions and evangelism. In fact, He will call many into radical evangelism.

Already, we have seen two or three remarkable miracles take place here in Toronto as the Lord has used young girls who have never before ministered in healing. This is a sign of what is to come. The average Christian who responds to the call of the Lion will be the initial giant killer.

But to whom much is given, much is required. In the outpouring of God's Spirit, the real revelation is not so much about dates and events as it is of God Himself. And just as the prophet was killed by the lion, we who respond to God will be called into accountability for what we do with the revelation of God.

This move of the Spirit in the Nineties is not just a charismatic or Pentecostal experience concerning power or gifting. It is one thing to be clothed with power, but it is another to be indwelt with the person of God. In the ministry times in Toronto, we have been encouraging people not just to get the experience but to soak in the presence of the Lord.

Where Is the Fruit?

Matthew 21 is a very important chapter for understanding end-time restoration, since it covers Jesus' final trip to Jerusalem. We are, in fact, living in a time when Jesus' Spirit wants to overturn the tables of Church life and turn the Church into a house of prayer. I am convinced that if we truly want to see a powerful move of the Holy Spirit in the Western world, we must learn to seek His face. God's mighty outpouring will not come until we pray.

But prayer is not the only task for this hour. If we look at verses 17-20, we see that Jesus, after leaving the Temple, the miracles, and the worship of the children, went to Bethany to spend the night. *Bethany*, in the Hebrew, means "house of figs." Figs signified peace and prosperity. The juice of figs was also used on occasion for medicinal purposes. The fig tree is unusual in that unlike most fruit trees, the fruit precedes the leaf. So Jesus, seeing the leaves, walked up to the tree and expected to find fruit. In His disappointment, He then cursed the fig tree, which rapidly withered.

Jesus said of the Father, in John 15:2 (NIV), "He cuts off every branch in Me that bears no fruit, while every branch that does bear fruit He prunes so that it will be even more fruitful." Many churches are like fig trees with leaves—having all the promise but no real nourishment for those who are thirsty and hungry. I believe God will soon increase judgment on churches and ministries that have all the programs and talk but fail to bear the fruit: seeing lives healed and transformed by God's Spirit.

As Jeremiah rebuked the leaders in Jeremiah 6:14 (NIV), "They dress the wound of My people as though it were not serious. 'Peace, peace,' they say, when there is no peace." At a time when God is going forth like a mighty warrior with a shout against His enemies (see Is. 42:13), He is taking very seriously leaders who are more concerned with maintaining the status quo and protecting their positions and reputations than in calling out to Him, "Not my will, but Yours, Father, ...whatever the cost."

When the Lion Roars

In numerous meetings since mid-1994, some people have been literally roaring as lions as the Spirit of God comes on them. Such unusual behavior is particularly difficult for the natural and/or the religious mind to put into perspective, since the manifestation is somewhat similar to that seen in demonized people. The difference, however, is these people exhibit no demonic anger or agony. Instead, a boldness and jealousy for God is in evidence. I believe this boldness is a prophetic manifestation of the fierceness with which the Lord is pursuing the lost and hurting.

Like everything else God does, people's flesh often tries to imitate it, and satan tries to counterfeit it. This is where spiritual discernment is specifically needed.

It seems the roaring mainly comes on those church leaders, evangelists, intercessors, or those in ministries who have multi-church ministries. No doubt this manifestation causes a wide array of reaction and criticism; but as I see it, these are the Father's children imitating by the Holy Spirit what the Lord is doing in the heavenlies.

One of the criticisms will be a typical pharisaic line: "I've never seen this before, so it can't be of God." One would think we want our Lion of Judah to be predictable and tame! To quote the characters in C.S. Lewis's Chronicles of Narnia whenever Aslan the lion (a Jesus figure) unexpectedly appeared and did unpredictable things, "Well, he's not really a tame lion, you know."

This, in essence, is the revelation the Bride of Christ needs today. Our Savior, the Lamb of God, is also the Lion of the tribe of Judah, the King of kings and Lord of lords. He is not a God we can completely understand or be comfortable with. Our comfort is to come from the Holy Comforter, but that flows out of relationship with Him, not by us trying to be in control of our situation.

The contemporary Church needs to understand that there are more promises in the Bible for those who fear God than there are for those who love Him. This does not detract from the fact that God is love and He always deals with His children in love. Even so, God deals with us not only in love, but also in truth. Psalm 85:10 (NIV) says, "Love and faithfulness meet together; righteousness and peace kiss each other." Just as truth without love is deadly, so love without the truth is a false or shallow love.

The Father seeks those who will worship in Spirit and in truth. The fruit of what the Spirit is currently doing is, as Philippians 2:12-13 (NIV) says, peoples' willingness to work out their "...salvation with fear and trembling, for it is God who works in you to will and to act according to His good purpose." We need a revelation that God is not the great "I WAS," or the "I WILL BE," but right here, right now, He is the great I AM.

The Best Is for Last

This lesson is taught throughout much of the Bible: The best is often last. Examples include: Haggai's prophecy that the latter glory would be greater than the former, Jesus' first miracle where, at the end of a wedding party, He created wine that was much better than what was served first, and Abraham's and Sarah's having promises from God fulfilled at a time when they thought old age had rendered the promises dead.

In Revelation 1, the apostle John, who in his life seemingly saw everything there is to see this side of Heaven, came into probably the greatest revelation of Jesus as Lord of the Church that anyone had ever experienced. After years of seeing the gospel touch most of the known world, after seeing the Mount of Transfiguration, the Ascension, and all the miracles of Jesus, as well as what he and the other disciples had done, John was imprisoned on the island of Patmos.

Much of the Church in the West today has an "island" mentality, which keeps us locked up. We are afraid to go out and touch our neighborhoods and workplaces with the reality of God's love. Although there is so much fear in the Church of the antichrist, the New Age movement, cults, etc., I believe that the biggest revelation of Jesus and His glory as it touches the world will come in these last days.

Isaiah 42:13,16 (NIV) says, "The Lord will march out like a mighty man, like a warrior He will stir up His zeal; with a shout He will raise the battle cry and will triumph over His enemies. ... I will lead the blind by ways they have not known, along unfamiliar paths I will guide them; I will turn the darkness into light before them and make the rough places smooth. These are the things I will do; I will not forsake them."

Chapter Nine

The Nineties in Perspective

From the mid-point of the Nineties, January 1995, I would like to relate four words (or visions) concerning churches in the Western world, Japan, Great Britain, and Germany. The first is a general word of encouragement for churches that have made a priority of seeking the Lord and being obedient to the leading of His Spirit, rather than being controlled by methodology or tradition. The succeeding three words are specifically for churches in Great Britain, Germany, and Japan, respectively. The time frame for these three visions was approximately 18 to 24 months, beginning mid-1994 for England and January 1, 1995, for Japan and Germany.

Birth Pangs

Contained in both the Bible and contemporary prophecies is the promise of a major move of God. This will be a move which, in both scope and power, will surpass any the Church has ever seen. It will be the fulfillment of Joel's promise of a time when the Spirit would be poured out on all mankind (see Joel 2:28), of Haggai's prophecy of a second time when God would shake the nations (see Hag. 2:7), of Jesus' prophecy that His believers would do even "greater works" than what He had done (see Jn. 14:12), of His prophetic prayer to the Father in John 17:17-23 that the Church would be perfected in unity, and of Jesus' prophecy in Matthew 24 that the time would come when the gospel would be preached to all nations, or ethnic groups (see Mt. 24:14).

Several, if not all these passages, seem to point to an end-time move of the Holy Spirit. For example, Joel's prophecy was interpreted by Peter on the day of Pentecost as being a last-days' event. If, as Peter believed, the last days began almost 2,000 years ago, how much more are we truly in the last days of the last days?

Some would argue that the "greater works" prophecy has already been fulfilled in the ministries of men like Billy Graham. But the words Jesus used in John 14 for "greater works"—the same as those used in John 5:20—specifically refer to miraculous works. Although healings and miracles are on the increase, the time has not yet come when believers are performing "greater works." Neither has the time arrived when the Body of Christ is truly united around what the Spirit is saying and doing.

Over the past 20 years or so, God has used many key voices to speak prophetically to the Body of Christ. These point to an incredible end-time move of the

Lord's Spirit. So that we might recognize this movement, we can identify three chief characteristics.

First, a massive flood of people from all nations will come to Christ. It is safe to say, based on Joel 2:28, this end-time move of the Spirit will make the same basic impact on every neighborhood, city, school, and workplace as Jesus and His disciples made for three-and-a-half years throughout the nation of Israel. Before the Lord's return, every individual will be confronted by the Kingdom of God in such a way as to be forced to make a conscious decision concerning Jesus. As at the trial of Jesus, people will either be His disciples or they will be adamantly against Him. Only this time, the world will be on trial and Jesus will be the judge.

Second, this end-time move of God's Spirit will be a demonstration not only of God's sovereignty and power but also of His incredible compassion. The promise of John 14:12 will be fulfilled, with miracles, signs, and wonders becoming commonplace. Blind eyes seeing, the lame walking, the deaf hearing, etc., will be more the norm than the exception as the gospel begins to powerfully touch the lost and hurting.

This is already true in a few areas such as Nagaland, India, where healings are already a way of life rather than being anomalies. The main problem I see in the cessationist's argument (which holds that because the Bible is canonized and the first apostles are gone, healings, signs, and wonders have ceased) is that God is the same yesterday, today, and forever. He is the same God now who healed then out of compassion for the lost and hurting (see Mt. 20:32-34). There has never been a time in Church history when healing has ceased, especially in diseased and exhaustion-ridden areas of the world.

Our God is moving in great power through His disciples. During this end-time move, John 14:12 will be fulfilled.

In keeping with Joel's promise of a prophetic time for men and women, young and old, I believe John 14:12 will be experienced by much of the end-time Church, regardless of denomination. This will not be a movement for just a few superstars. Already in Toronto, teenagers who have never before moved in the Spirit have been touched by the renewal. Amazingly, they are beginning to move in strong healings and evangelism.

Last, many churches will see their denominational walls break down. This is not to say that churches will lose their uniqueness. On the contrary, just as Elijah built the altar on Mount Carmel with 12 stones, one for each of the 12 tribes, the end-time move of God will be made up of churches unique in their God-given distinctions.

For the purpose of taking cities for Christ, churches will come together for prayer and worship in a unity centered around the leading of the Holy Spirit. As leaders begin to get a bigger revelation of God's glory and holiness, and we begin to get the Father's heart for one another, we will begin to understand that our uniqueness can be no cause for pride or walls. It is only in unity that our uniqueness can come together to complement one another.

The time is drawing near—and, in fact, in some cities is already here—for churches to come together and fill arenas and halls with prayer and worship.

Bringing in the First Fruits

The real move of the end-time harvest is still some eight to ten years away for most cities in the Western world. As in the time of John the Baptist, we are going through a period of prophetic restoration of our hearts and lives in preparation for the move of the Lamb of God.

Interestingly, although many churches are unable to get enough volunteers for their own Sunday school programs, they feel ready to reap an end-time harvest. For them, the perspective of "If you can't do it in Jerusalem, you're not ready for Samaria" is good to keep in mind. Many of us need to be recaptured by God's love. We need to return to the place where our hearts are totally abandoned to God's will and purposes.

Those who are seriously seeking first the Kingdom of God and responding to the Holy Spirit are, metaphorically speaking, already immersed in the Jordan. Historically, entering into the Jordan symbolizes two truths: change or repentance, as with John the Baptist's ministry; and entering into the promises of God, as with the Hebrews crossing the Jordan.

In general, like the River of Life described in Ezekiel 47, the current move of the Holy Spirit (what some call the "Toronto Blessing") is the River of Life at the ankle level—bringing spiritual refreshment. This is not to say there is any sort of elite group of people, such as those who have traveled to Toronto or have been touched by the manifestations. The Holy Spirit moves and speaks through a myriad of ways. No matter His method, God is speaking, refreshing, and anointing many right now. It is critical that we respond to Him in His perfect timing, regardless of how He chooses to speak.

The first level of the River of Life is only ankle deep. That may not seem like much when compared with the fourth and final stage, where Ezekiel could not ford the river because of the strength and depth of the water. Nonetheless, the feet, covered by ankle-deep water, are symbolic of taking forward the good news (see Is. 52:7; Lk. 9:5; and Eph. 6:15).

The 12 spies who initially crossed into the Promised Land brought back not only a report of what they saw and experienced but also tangible evidence. Numbers 13:23 (NIV) reads, "When they reached the Valley of Eshcol, they cut off a branch bearing a single cluster of grapes. Two of them carried it on a pole between them, along with some pomegranates and figs."

In like manner, I believe many who respond to the Spirit of God and get wet in the now-flowing River of Life will have a new freedom and anointing throughout the decade; they will be the ones to bring back the first fruits. Even though we are still several years away from the culturally transforming renewals, such as some

Third World countries are experiencing, the first fruits are now going to become visible, and as with the 12 spies, they will come in heavy bunches.

Without going into more detail at this point, I will say that everything the Lord has been speaking to me concerning the decade of the Nineties has to do with God's mercy and compassion toward hurting and desperate people who do not really know Him at this time.

A Word for the British Isles
(First publicly released in London, June 1994)

I believe this is a word for the Anglicans of Great Britain and also for the larger Body of Christ in the British Isles.

The Lord showed me a vision of a large traditional church building. It could have been anywhere in Great Britain. The walls were of stone and natural-colored brick, and it had a slate roof. Tremendous winds began to blow ferociously against the church.

(As an aside, it is important to keep in mind that the word for *Spirit* in the Hebrew is the word *ruwach*, which means "wind" or "breath;" it can also mean a "violent exhalation." In Acts 2:2 (KJV), prior to the disciples' preaching of the gospel to the city of Jerusalem, the Holy Spirit came over them as a "rushing mighty wind." This was clearly a different experience than John 20:22, when Jesus first breathed on the disciples.)

As the winds reached their heaviest, the four walls of the church building were completely blown away to the point that one could not even see any debris. Despite the building's collapse, the hand of the Lord held up the roof, which did not move. The four missing walls of brick began to be replaced by glass walls, which were completely transparent but strong enough to support the roof.

As this transition was taking place, two things happened. One, the people inside the church began to see the people outside quite clearly. That is to say, they began to see the world through the eyes of God. Many people in the church who had never had a burden for the lost and hurting began to go out and minister God's love to those outside and bring them into the Kingdom of God.

At the same time, people outside the church, such as passersby and church neighbors, began to see into the church and see the reality of God among His people. Most of these people had avoided the church in the past because they assumed that Christians were just "quaint, religious people" who were out of touch with reality. I believe the Lord showed me that in 1995, He had begun a process of renewal in many churches throughout Great Britain and was preparing them for the work of the harvest.

A Word for Japan
(First released publicly in September 1994)

In another vision, I saw tremendous winds and waves—Tsunami storms—hitting the nation of Japan. I believe the Lord was showing me how the nation was going to be shaken economically, politically, physically, and even spiritually. The period during which the winds and waves hitting the islands was approximately 18 months.

I saw an increase in political scandals and the *yen* plunging into deeper problems. The one overwhelming message the Lord gave me for Japan was that God loves the Japanese too much to leave them as they are; the only thing that would wake them up from the idolatry of money and pride was a national shaking on all fronts. I even saw the nation being shaken geographically with mighty winds, waves, and earthquakes.

One week after I first saw this vision, in the early autumn, the news reported a huge storm in Japan that had killed a dozen people or so.

I believe the fruits of this overall storm of 18 months will be in two areas. One, the churches and Christians who are actively seeking the Lord for their nation will experience a tremendous move as in the day of Pentecost. There will be a new boldness as many Christians step past cultural barriers and talk to fellow Japanese about Jesus. Also, there will be a greater freedom in some of the churches for healings and miracles to take place.

Second, because of these natural disasters, many Japanese who have been closed to Jesus because of pride, false religion, and materialism will be shaken and afraid for the future. They will become more open to the gospel and will respond.

The world will take notice when this happens, for Japan has been notoriously difficult for the gospel to penetrate.

Author's Note: Since the date of this prophecy, Japan has experienced a major earthquake (killing over 4,000 people) and cultic terrorist activity that caused death and chaos on Japan's train systems due to a highly lethal, poisonous gas. Further, confidence in Japan's once powerful economic structure has been mightily shaken, despite the strenth of the yen against the dollar.

A Word for Germany
(First released in December 1994)

In the third vision, I saw vast fields of wheat ripe for the harvest. Gentle summer breezes of God's Spirit continually blew, causing the wheat to be flexible and to move according to the direction of the wind. The summer sun shone beautifully on the fields.

Not many, perhaps ten percent of the workers needed, were out beginning to work the fields. But there was such a joy on these workers, that even though they were few in number, they were singing, dancing, and celebrating the work and harvest as they went about it. This joy they experienced in the Spirit of the Lord gave them great strength to do the work. Like the Gadites who chose to fight with David, "the least was a match for a hundred, and the greatest for a thousand."

Provoked by Jealousy

In the account of Gideon's initial victory against the Midianites and the Amalekites, God started with just

300 men against possibly 60,000 or more. Just the camels of the Midianites and the Amalekites "could no more be counted than the sand on the seashore" (Judg. 7:12 NIV). The enemy soldiers were as "thick as locusts." When Gideon first began to have success, three other tribes, the Naphtali, Asher, and Manasseh, were quick to join in. Then one of the leading tribes, Ephraim, also joined and was powerfully used by the Lord.

These other tribes were provoked by jealousy into joining what the Lord was doing. Even as a little bit of salt makes the whole salty, so a few churches entering into the first fruits will, in a healthy way, provoke other churches and leaders into entering in. This is a good jealousy, rather than a carnal one. It is a hunger that leads us into God's will and breaks pride and complacency.

Year of Jubilee

1995 marks the fiftieth anniversary of the end of World War II. There have been many prophetic words concerning the obvious jubilee-year comparison, especially for Germany. The jubilee year was a time for slaves to be given freedom and debts to be canceled. The analogy for Germany, England, and Japan is quite strong. These nations were not only three of the principal players involved in the fighting, but they were also greatly devastated by the war.

The time is here not only for the cancellation of debts, as Christians intercede and seek forgiveness, but for renewal. This, in fact, has already begun in many churches; the first fruits of revival are ripening in the world's cultures.

In describing my vision of the harvest workers in Germany, I mentioned the Gadite warriors who joined David. First Chronicles 12:8 (NIV) states, "Their faces were the faces of lions." This is symbolic of the warriors who will be in the forefront of God's army. They will be those who have experienced a revelation of Jesus as not only the Lamb of God but also as the Lion of the tribe of Judah.

Concerning these Gadite warriors, First Chronicles 12:15 (NIV) also says, "It was they who crossed the Jordan in the first month when it was overflowing all its banks, and they put to flight everyone living in the valleys, to the east and to the west." Just as John was baptizing people in preparation for the coming of the Lamb of God, the outpouring that began in 1993 to 1994 is a baptism into the River of Life (which is mentioned in Ezekiel 47 and Revelation 22). Those who respond to the current outpouring of the Holy Spirit before any more time elapses will be in the forefront of the workers of the coming harvest.

May God arise, may His enemies be scattered; may His foes flee before Him. As smoke is blown away by the wind, may You blow them away; as wax melts before the fire, may the wicked perish before God. But may the righteous be glad and rejoice before God; may they be happy and joyful. Sing to God, sing praise to His name, extol Him who rides on the clouds—His name is the Lord—and rejoice before Him. A father to the fatherless, a defender of widows, is God in His holy dwelling. God sets the lonely in families, He leads forth the prisoners with singing; but the rebellious live in a sun-scorched land. When You went out before Your people, O God, when You marched through the wasteland, the earth shook, the heavens poured down rain, before God, the One of Sinai, before God, the God of Israel. You gave abundant showers, O God; You refreshed Your weary inheritance. Your people settled in it, and from Your bounty, O God, You provided for the poor. The Lord announced the word, and great was the company of those who proclaimed it (Psalm 68:1-11 NIV).

Final Note

Again, I am not speaking of an elite group who have been to the Toronto Airport Vineyard Church or anywhere else in particular. Neither am I referring to those who may have experienced a manifestation. I am speaking of those who are crying out to God, laying down their lives, and praying, "Father, Your will, not mine."

Chapter Ten

A Season of Transition

One of the words the Lord has been speaking repeatedly to me, as well as to many others, is *transition*. Late in the winter of 1996, the Lord spoke repeatedly to me concerning the summer of '96 and the next few years. The basic message was that this would be a major season of transition for many churches and leaders in the Body of Christ. *Transition*, according to Roget's Thesaurus means to be "converted or changed." *Transitional* means "convertible."

In the early Eighties a church was planted in Kansas City, Missouri, by a young couple by the name of Mike and Diane Bickle. As the church grew, it became a haven for the fresh emergence of prophetic ministry. In addition to this strong regard for the prophetic, the church also focused on intercessory prayer, worship, and missions. For several years many of the church members met daily, seven days a week, in order to pray for revival to come to North America.

In 1982, while in Cairo, Egypt, Mike Bickle received a very strong word from the Lord. The gist of it was that in one generation (Mike's generation) the Lord would change the understanding and expression of Christianity to the world. The Lord was not saying that doctrine or theology would change; there is basically no new biblical doctrine or theology. However, to the world, the lost, their understanding of Christ and the expression of the Christ through the Church would take on a whole new vitality.

Even without saying new doctrine or theology is coming, this is a very threatening word for many leaders. It is threatening in the same way that the religious leaders of Jesus' time were threatened by His ministry. It was not so much that new things were happening, but that the power and freedom of God was being manifested in ways that simply did not fit within their traditions. The fact is that the leaders of Jesus' day put as much of an emphasis on the Talmud as they did the Torah. This is to say, they emphasized their traditions as much as the writings of Moses and the prophets. Despite the fact that we teach so much theology in our evangelical churches, we often fall into the same trap today. Like the Pharisees of Jesus' day, many leaders automatically dismiss anything new that they have not previously experienced, or that they cannot completely understand intellectually.

I believe this prophecy of Bickle's to be of importance because it is necessary for us to understand how much we need to be flexible before the Lord in order to come to a place where a true biblical expression of Christ can come through the Church to the lost. For the present-day Church to experience what took place in the early Church of Jerusalem, we very much need to have our tables turned over.

The thought of our lives or situations being quickly changed by God can be hard to put into perspective. This is especially true if we do not understand God's sovereign intervention. Christians need to understand that life with God requires joint participation. As disciples, we are called to active obedience. The Bible clearly states that we reap what we sow. On God's part, however, He does not merely move or act in response to our actions or prayers. Because He is *sovereign*, He often moves in our lives, situations, and cultures according to His sovereign will and timing. As Nebuchadnezzar, the heathen king of Babylon, proclaimed of the Lord God Jehovah, "...His dominion is an eternal dominion; His kingdom endures from generation to generation. All the peoples of the earth are regarded as nothing. He does as He pleases with the powers of heaven and the peoples of the earth. No one can hold back His hand or say to Him: 'What have You done?' " (Dan. 4:34-35 NIV)

Chosen Times

There are times the Bible calls *kairos* or *chosen* times when God acts beyond our expectations and sometimes our understanding. The entire culture or nation is changed by God's Spirit as in the times of Elijah or John the Baptist. The prophet Isaiah spoke of such a time in Isaiah 42 when God would speak new things, give new songs, and go forth as a mighty warrior.

It is critical to realize that such times tend to create problems for much of the Church: problems in that the sheer sovereignty of God's hand in motion removes us from our comfort zones; problems in that, despite our theology, we like feeling that we are in control and completely understand what is up and what is down; problems in that God often wreaks havoc with our sense of religious control and traditions when He turns over our tables and rearranges the order. In short, the problem with a God on the move is the age-old issue of pharisaism.

The essence of pharisaism is twofold: (1) God can do nothing that we have not previously experienced, and (2) God will do nothing that we can not completely understand. Pharisaism always rears its ugly head when God is about to move beyond our understanding, our control, or our comfort zones.

The problems first begin to surface with the prophetic proclamation of what's to come. Amos 3:7 (NIV) states that God "does nothing without revealing His plan to His servants the prophets." The first tremors begin with prophetic words to the Church that the status quo is about to change.

Most of Matthew 23 is basically a scathing, haranguing rebuke of the Pharisees and Sadducees. In verse 37 Jesus poignantly reveals His heart concerning Jerusalem's pharisaic rejection of Him. He grieves over the fact that the people always stone His messengers. Three verses later, in chapter 24 (see also Mk. 13:1), His disciples are remarking on the beauty and grandeur of the Temple building. The very thing that was used to attack and destroy the prophetic (stones) was also used to build the Temple, Israel's greatest religious monument.

When King David envisioned the Temple and prepared his son Solomon to build it, he never intended it to become an idol or a system to replace an immediate relationship with God. David realized that the true sacrifice the Lord wanted was not bulls, goats, and pigeons used by the priests in the Temple. Rather, God wanted hearts that were broken and contrite before Him and searching after Him (see Ps. 51). Isaiah 66:1-2 states that God's true resting place is within people who are broken and humble before Him, as opposed to things we can build with human hands.

It was a beautiful place of worship and prayer that David had directed Solomon to build, but over the years it had been reduced to a mere monument of mechanized prayer and rituals. The point Jesus was making, however, was that Israel's greatest religious monument was composed of what always attacked the prophetic. He prophesied that because Israel was not recognizing the time of her visitation, not one stone of the existing structure would be left standing on another.

A Time of Transition and Judgment

Transition (or change) can be very upsetting because we humans tend to be creatures of habit. Being transitional necessitates being able to embrace change despite being ruffled or shaken by the process. Jesus equated those led by the Spirit to the wind: "...you hear the sound of it, but do not know where it comes from and where it is going..." (Jn. 3:8). Life is always about growth, which requires change—not a change of eternal values and truth, but a change in focus and perspective as we grow in relationship with ourselves, others, and especially God, *especially* during a *kairos* time. Again, as Isaiah 42 reads: "Behold, the former things have come to pass, now I declare new things..." (Is. 42:9).

As Psalm 68 reads, when God's presence goes forth, the earth quakes and the rains come to the parched lands. Often, like on the day of Pentecost, a new release of authority and power comes to some of God's servants. But, it can also be a time of judgment on the religious leaders and the institutions in which they might trust. This is illustrated by the prophecy of Matthew 23.

In July of 1996, the Lord gave me a very clear vision of a temple building. Probably, because of its vastness, it was the Temple built during the time of Herod, as opposed to Solomon's. The limestone blocks of the outer walls were huge. The craft work was impressive in that all these huge stones fit together perfectly. In the picture, the sunlight was playing brilliantly on the outer walls. The walls glinted with different hues of yellow, gold, white, and grey. What stood out the most, however, was the sheer size and magnificence.

The Lord made it clear that this temple represented the "church made by hands" as opposed to one built by

His Spirit. The building represented a great respectability and a love of tradition. It represented idolatry of what we can establish in our own strength. It symbolized all that the Church leans to as opposed to the freedom and leading of the Holy Spirit.

The winds (*ruwach*) of the Spirit began to breath on this building. At first the winds were rather gentle, but continually and gradually they increased to the point where the building was knocked down. Just as the actual Temple was destroyed according to Jesus' prophecy, in the vision not one stone was left on another. The beauty and majesty of the man-made institution was gone.

As the dust settled, what was visible, besides the destruction, was a great multitude of people. These were God's people, Christians who began to experience and realize the freedom of the Spirit in a greater degree. They began to understand that true worship and obedience could not be contained or measured by method or dogma. They realized that the Holy Spirit was calling them into a new dimension of freedom and power to know, worship, and represent Christ.

"Do You Not See All These Things"

The manifestations of the Holy Spirit are often very upsetting to many. Loud laughter, shaking and falling down, drunkenness in the Spirit, and roaring as a lion, do not fit at all into our religious bastions of respectability. However, offending our religious thinking patterns is definitely part of God's purpose in this move of the Spirit. Just as Jesus' style of ministry was offensive to the leaders of His day, so it is with the Holy Spirit's moving today. We can forget too easily that the freedom to know God came at Calvary, but the power to represent Him came in the upper room on Pentecost. The release of Pentecost is as confusing and offensive in today's Church as it was for the Jews in Jerusalem.

The very heart of the gospel message is offensive. Paul said in First Corinthians 1:18a (NIV): "For the message of the cross is foolishness to those who are perishing." Jesus spoke in parables due to the dullness of the hearts of the people. Isaiah referred to the prophetic things as a "a stone of stumbling and a rock of offense" (1 Pet. 2:8). Jesus Himself, being the true cornerstone, is the "stone which the builders rejected" (Mk. 12:10).

God moves in ways that deliberately challenge our religious and traditional views in order to provoke the heart. God is love, after all, and the greatest commandment is to love first with all our hearts, before our minds. God often offends the mind in order to reveal the heart. Nowhere are we as easily shaken as by the thought that *our* status quo may no longer be God's status quo. We are a race of beings that, in general, are very resistant to change. Nowhere do we tend to be more dogmatic regarding our traditions than in religious structures. Barthelemy wrote, "I pity the man who, proud of his system, says 'My ideas have not changed for 30 years. I am what I was, I love what I loved.' The ridiculous man is he who never changes." As stated earlier, I am not referring to change of biblical doctrine, but rather of our ways of expressing Christ to the world.

The invitation into transition during the days of Jesus' ministry in Israel was of monumental proportions. It was not only the recognition of the true Messiah but also an invitation into a new covenant with God. As Jeremiah prophesied hundreds of years earlier:

"This is the covenant I will make with the house of Israel after that time," declares the Lord. "I will put My law in their minds and write it on their hearts. I will be their God, and they will be My people. No longer will a man teach his neighbor, or a man his brother, saying, 'Know the Lord,' because they will all know Me, from the least of them to the greatest," declares the Lord (Jeremiah 31:33 NIV).

No longer would the law be something on a scroll, or a tablet of stone. By His Spirt, the living God would now dwell within the hearts of His people. The paramount importance of responding to that invitation was reflected in the consequence of rejecting the invitation. Basically, it meant destruction for the Temple and much of the way of life for the Hebrew people in the years to come.

There are in a parallel way, if not of quite the same importance, times in Church history when God has invited His people to respond to a new move of His Spirit. Those times can often be thought of as *kairos* times—times when God is moving quite sovereignly in great power beyond what we have seen before. Historically, when the status quo resists that invitation, the consequences are real. We can offend the Holy Spirit in a similar way to how Jerusalem grieved Jesus. This is not to say that a truly born-again Christian can lose his salvation by not responding to the prophetic. But it was Jesus Himself who told the church of Laodicea that if they did not buy from Him gold refined by fire, He would reveal their nakedness to the world. As Paul stated, Christians can quench, or grieve, the Holy Spirit when they despise the prophetic speaking of God to His people. Paul also wrote, "For all who are being led by the Spirit of God, these are sons of God" (Rom. 8:14). It is of paramount importance for the contemporary Church to respond to the leading of the Holy Spirit today if we are going to see real revival break out.

"Do you not see all these things?" Jesus asked His disciples, in Matthew 24:2. They had just finished commenting on the beauty of the Temple building. In Mark 13:1-2 (NIV) there is a similar passage: "As He was leaving the temple, one of His disciples said to Him, 'Look, Teacher! What massive stones! What magnificent buildings!' 'Do you see all these great buildings?' replied Jesus. 'Not one stone here will be left on another; every one will be thrown down.' " The disciples, not unlike many Christians today, had a hard time putting everything that was happening into perspective because of a fascination with the outward religious monument of the status quo.

There can be great value in observing the traditions and practices that are prevalent in our different denominations. Quite often tradition can be seen as a stepping-stone from revivals in the past to revivals in the future. Certainly, there was a wonderful history attached to the Temple building. But when the structure, or practices, of a church take on more importance than the leading of the Holy Spirit, those traditions become a demonic stronghold over the people of God. We can come to the point where we are more concerned with maintaining the status quo than with seeking first the Kingdom of God.

When that fixation with our systems causes us to grieve the Spirit, there can be consequences. Owen Hendrix is credited with the following quote: "These are seven last words of many churches: 'We never did it this way before.' " Church history is filled with stories of churches that blazed with revival fire only to see those fires dwindle into little more than occasional sparks in one generation or less. A classic example is the famous Church of Hampton of the "Great Awakening" revival. Under Jonathan Edward's leadership the church moved in three waves of revival between 1734 and 1750. After 17 years of incredible history, the church booted out Edwards in a dispute about communion. In the span of a few years, that church fell into obscurity. It lost most of the potential fruit and momentum of the revival that had dramatically touched much of the existing Church on the eastern seaboard.

The question the Lord Jesus asks many of us today is no different than what He said to His disciples regarding the Temple. Do we not see all these things the Holy Spirit is doing in these days? Can we step outside our own fascination with our ways of doing things to see the bigger picture? Is it possible that God does have more for our times than we have seen, more than we have heard, and more than has entered into our understandings? In the last 20 years there have been more real conversions to Christ than in the preceding 2000. The breakthroughs that have come in the last 25 years concerning prayer, deliverance, the importance of small groups, spiritual gifts for the whole Body, worship, etc., are nothing short of phenomenal. The prophetic words to the Church are overwhelmingly centered around revival and God's heart for the nations.

Still, especially in North America and the rest of the Western world, there is almost overwhelming resistance to revival, not so much from without the Church, but from within. The power of pharisaism, the stronghold of the religious spirit, cannot be underestimated. The religious spirit stems from the antichrist. The antichrist is, obviously, against Christ, the accomplishment of the cross, and what His future intentions are. To the true Christian, satan, as with Adam and Eve, cannot convincingly say "God does not exist." But the spirit of religion may be successful in convincing us to have a dogmatic faith in our own understandings of how God can work. This is the trap of pharisaism.

In August of 1996, the Lord spoke to me concerning September 14, the day of Rosh Hashanah according to the Hebrew civil calender. Rosh Hashanah is the Jewish New Year. According to the Hebrew religious calendar, September 14, 1996, was actually Yom Teruah, or "the Day of Trumpets." This is what Paul refers to in First Corinthians 15:52 when he speaks of Christ's return, saying "in the twinkling of an eye, at the last trump."

The Lord indicated that there would be a fresh release of Kingdom authority for many of His leaders and servants who were seeking after Him. But He also indicated that judgment would be released for many who were fighting and resisting the Spirit in the name of clinging to their own "orthoproxies" or ways of doing things. In short, I felt as if the Lord was saying "enough is enough"! Just as the consequences were real for those who staunchly resisted Jesus, I believe that the consequences will be real for those Church leaders who stubbornly refuse to humble themselves before the Lord.

We have an opportune time before us—a window of opportunity, so to speak, to move into a fresh expression of Christ. Revival or *kairos* times are before the Church. If, however, we prefer to cling to our religious monuments of the past, we will, in effect, use those very things to attack the prophetic leading of the Holy Spirit.

We, the people of God, are the living stones that are to be fitted together by the Holy Spirit into a house of God (see 1 Pet. 2). We, corporately—not in the work of our hands, our traditions, or our practices— are the house the Lord wants to build. The house the Lord is after is a Church "not made with hands," at least not our hands (see 2 Cor. 5:1). But like in the time of Jesus' triumphal entry into Jerusalem, God will raise up "rocks" out in the world for His purposes, if we don't stand up and worship Him with a fresh passion.

This is what the Lord says: "Heaven is My throne, and the earth is My footstool. Where is the house you will build for Me? Where will My resting place be? Has not My hand made all these things, and so they came into being?" declares the Lord. "This is the one I esteem: he who is humble and contrite in spirit, and trembles at My word" (Isaiah 66:1-2 NIV).

Chapter Eleven

The Dancing Bride of Christ

We are in an age in which it seems that knowledge is replacing life itself. With videos, computers, and the arrival of virtual reality, many are becoming increasingly isolated. As our Western world culture is becoming more centered on knowledge, relationships, ostensibly, are becoming more and more utilitarian. We see in society as a whole a growing trend toward fragmentation of differing ethnic groups, ages, and genders.

Experts say that real knowledge is now doubling every two years. The problem is that an individual's capacity to reason has not increased. Possibly the fruit of this increased technology is not only group isolation but individual alienation in one's own culture. A heartless and computer-dominated future, as depicted by science fiction movies of the Fifties and Sixties, is subtly coming to pass.

Over the past few years God has been doing something completely fresh in the midst of many congregations—something that is very experiential as it releases truth to the heart, beyond the mere thought process. The Father is playing with His children, and Jesus is romancing His Bride. These can be hard concepts for many to grasp. God *playing* with His children—what's the point? *Jesus* a *romantic*—get real!

By now several good books are available to help people understand the laughter, joy, drunkenness, and other manifestations that have been taking place. I recommend John Arnott's *The Father's Blessing*; Guy Chevreau's *Catch the Fire*; Dave Roberts' *The Toronto Blessing*; and Dr. Mark Stibbe's *Times of Refreshing*. The problem, however, still remains: Head knowledge, in itself, can open up a person neither to the heart of God nor the thoughts of God.

To suggest there is a strong part of God that is irrational sounds like heresy to many. From human understanding, however, or the lack thereof, there is the motivation of God that makes no sense. *God is love*, according to First John 4:8. Pure, passionate, unadulterated love is something that often defies logic and, indeed, sometimes throws it out the window. Love, rather than only truth or pure cold logic, is the reason why God created and redeemed man, why He desires, by His Spirit, to enter an intimate relationship with His children. Passion is the impetus of John 3:16: "for God so loved the world."

The Church too often resembles the Greeks or Gentiles Paul referred to in First Corinthians 1:22-23, who look for wisdom. The cross was and is a stumbling block to both Jews and Gentiles alike because God's love only makes sense to someone who is desperate, or to another passionate lover.

The Song of Solomon—A Picture of God and His People

God has often illustrated His heart by metaphorically comparing His people to a bride for Himself. At least twice the prophet Jeremiah painted Israel as an unfaithful wife. In the powerful story of Hosea marrying a prostitute who then went back to her old lifestyle, God reveals the depths of His love for His people. The apostle Paul, the foremost theologian of the New Testament, described the mystery of the Church and Jesus as being like a man and a woman in marriage.

One of the most poignant pictures God gives of His heart for His people is the Song of Solomon. This book has been labeled by some as "God's erotic poetry" concerning the joy of sexual intimacy between a husband and wife. One sixteenth century Spanish scholar was actually imprisoned four years for translating the book from Hebrew into Spanish. It is often used by counselors and teachers concerning marriage and sex. As helpful as the writings of Solomon may be in this respect, I believe that God was prophetically and poetically speaking through this allegory. He was painting a vivid picture with rich deep hues to help us understand His heart. Even the whole idea of man's and woman's need for emotional and physical intimacy is a picture of God's desire for relationship. Because man was made in God's image, a healthy marriage being consummated is, in the end, a picture of what will take place in the spirit between Jesus and His Bride—the Church.

According to First Kings 4:32, Solomon wrote over a thousand songs. Of all these songs, he chose this one to be called the "Song of Songs." To Solomon, this song of romance with a young Hebrew girl who was a worker in her brothers' vineyards was the greatest of all his songs.

The girl was darkened by the sun due to the extent of her work. (A strong tan in those times was not desirable. It was a sign of belonging to the lower class of laborers.) Evidently her workload from her brothers was so extensive that she was forced to neglect her own vineyard. Chapters 1 and 2 are basically about the king, Solomon, coming disguised as a shepherd, and romancing her. This is an illustration of Jesus, who had no stately form or majesty in appearance, coming for humanity. He came because of His love for a bride who was laden with deep troubles and burdens. In chapters 3 and 4, we read of the king revealing his true identity and wedding the girl. Chapters 5–8 describe the testing and working out of that love.

Of all the books in the Bible, probably none portrays God in a greater way as a true romantic in His love for us. And of this book, conceivably no section is more poignant than chapter 5, verse 28. This passage demonstrates both the grief we can cause the Lord when we ignore His advances, as well as the price we pay for neglecting Him.

The Wooing of the Holy Spirit

Song of Songs 5:2-8 tells the story of the bride, who at the end of the day has taken off her day clothes and put on her night garments. She has washed and fully prepared herself for bed. Her bridegroom, damp from the night air, comes for her and knocks on the locked door for her to open it. Unfortunately the bride is more concerned about keeping her nightly ritual than about responding to her heart and her lover. As her lover calls for her, she remarks that her heart is awake. It is not that she is completely insensitive to him, but rather that she failed to respond from her heart. Her bridegroom continues to ardently pursue her—speaking words of romance and trying to physically reach through the latticework by the door to undo the lock from the inside.

This heartbeat of the Lord for His lover, the Church, is also pictured in Revelation 3:14-21. This contains Jesus' address to the last of the seven churches—the church of Laodicea. Among other messages, I believe that each of the churches Jesus spoke to is somewhat symbolic of the church throughout the ages, with the church of Laodicea being symbolic of the end-time church. The church of Laodicea paints a picture of Christians who are filled with complacency and apathy, being lukewarm in their hunger and love for Jesus. They are filled up with themselves; they are self-satisfied. This is also the picture of the girl in Song of Songs, chapter 5. She knows that she loves her shepherd, that her heart is beating for her lover, yet she can't be bothered to get up out of the bed of her self-satisfaction.

Behold I Stand at the Door and Knock!

Just as the girl's lover stood at the door and knocked, so the Holy Spirit is knocking today for the Bride of Christ. "I stand at the door and knock" is often used in evangelistic messages to the unsaved, but Jesus, in Revelation 3:20, was addressing the Church. This is the prophetic stirring of the Spirit in the Church today, complete with joy, drunkenness, and power. Like a lover, He is wanting His Bride to be intoxicated and consumed with His love and His heart for the lost.

To our discredit, we often resemble the bride of Solomon. We can be more concerned with the traditions and rituals of our meetings than with waiting and responding to what the Holy Spirit wants to do or say. This is not to say, in any way whatsoever, that we should abandon or neglect the teaching and preaching of the Bible. The problem, however, is that we have so deeply focused our meetings on our conceptual knowledge of God that we often neglect the person of God.

My hero of the Bible, other than Jesus, is David—not because he killed Goliath or was a great soldier or king, but because of his unabashed passion for the person of God. In his love songs to God he writes:

...Thy lovingkindness is better than life (Psalm 63:3).

As the deer pants for the water brooks, so my soul pants for Thee, O God (Psalm 42:1).

"I cried out to Thee, O Lord; I said, Thou art My refuge, My portion in the land of the living" (Psalm 142:5).

In Second Samuel 6, we read of David dancing before the Ark out of sheer joy that the presence of God was coming to be with the people. David's heart for God was the reason, according to Samuel, God chose David, rather than Saul, to be the true king of Israel.

God Is a God of Order, But of *His* Order Not *Ours*

One of the greatest arguments against this move of the Spirit is that order is being thrown out the window. First Corinthians 14:33 (NIV) reads: "For God is not a God of disorder but of peace." The question does need to be asked, nevertheless: whose order? There is considerable arrogance in assuming that our order is necessarily God's order. The Bishop David Pytches of St. Anne's Church of Chorly Woods, England has put it this way: "The church should have order but the order of the family not the order of the factory." A factory is primarily concerned with putting out a product as quickly and efficiently as possible. God is primarily concerned with relationship. Consequently Jesus is very concerned that His Bride not merely know *about* Him, but genuinely know Him as a person and lover.

The order that God seems to be preferring in the Nineties is the new order that was established in Matthew 21 by turning over the tables and creating temporary mayhem. Although this brought confusion to the priests, nothing less would suffice to bring about God's desire that His house be a place of prayer, of communion with Him.

To those who would argue that we are to walk by faith not by experience, I would counter: Our faith is to lead to our experience of life in the Kingdom of God. As with the experience in the Temple when Jesus turned over the tables, perhaps God in His mercy is wanting to deliver us from our twentieth century predisposition for busyness—busyness that robs us of time for relationships with God and one another.

I am not saying that Christians should seek after either experience or manifestations; rather, we should seek Jesus. The point is that God is a God of relationship who draws near to those who draw near to Him. Sometimes His Spirit comes as a still gentle breeze and speaks to our hearts; other times He comes as a mighty rushing wind. God not only wants to speak to His children; He wants to fill them with His joy and power. We tend to be so lopsided in our equation of Christian life that there can be no room for God's presence. As David wrote in Psalm 16: "You have made known to me the path of life; You will fill me with joy in Your presence, with eternal pleasures at Your right hand" (Ps. 16:11 NIV).

What is God's goal for the Church in the years ahead? It's twofold I believe: (1) to bring about an increasing harvest of lost souls into His Kingdom, and (2) to prepare the Church, or the Bride of Christ, for the wedding to His Son Jesus. The Father deeply, deeply loves His Son. He is extremely proud of Him. Some might think that this can't be, that all pride is sin. But just as Paul wrote to the Christians at Corinth that he took great pride in them (see 2 Cor. 7:4), God the Father takes great pride in His Son, who honored Him and obeyed Him at great personal sacrifice. The foremost thing the Father is doing is preparing a Bride from the nations for His Son, with whom He is well pleased. (See Psalm 2.)

None of us wants to walk down the aisle with a bride (or bridegroom) who is filled with legalism and contention, who is self-willed and apathetic in her (or his) love. We are like Solomon's bride, stirred in our hearts for our lover, but still more concerned with our programs. We can, at times, greatly resemble the church of Laodicea—lukewarm in our love, rather than hot in our passion for God. God is attempting to raise us up out of the bed of complacency and self-satisfaction.

The Dancing Bride

In 1984 the Lord spoke to me out of Isaiah 61:3 (NIV): "and provide for those who grieve in Zion—to bestow on them a crown of beauty instead of ashes, the oil of gladness instead of mourning, and a garment of praise instead of a spirit of despair. They will be called oaks of righteousness, a planting of the Lord for the display of His splendor." Hence the name Mantle of Praise Ministries (KJV). I believe the Lord spoke to me at that time that the Spirit was going to take the Church much deeper into prayer, worship, intimacy, joy, and the power of the Lord.

In the autumn of 1994, the Lord spoke to me that the dancing days were coming to the Bride of Christ.

Dancing, as with laughter in Church, is often deeply frowned on as being mere emotional display or a religiously contrived fervor induced through manipulation or hype. Only the most stoic, emotionally void critic, however, would say that David's exuberant dancing in bringing the Ark into the city of David was not a deep down response of love to God. Zephaniah 3:17 reads: "The Lord your God is in your midst, a victorious warrior. He will exult over you with joy, He will be quiet in His love, He will rejoice over you with shouts of joy." There are times when God is evidently much more like David in His celebration than like our highly programmed and rigid church services.

Since the autumn of 1994, I have in fact been privileged to see some times of celebration that were possibly historical for their locality. In Jyleskia, Finland, in early 1995, I spoke at a conference with over 5,000 Finnish Christians from every single denomination in Finland. On several of the nights, there were hundreds of people dancing and greatly rejoicing in the Spirit. Several pastors were in tears as they witnessed what they had thought was impossible—different denominational Christians dancing and worshiping God with abandonment. As 1995 progressed, I saw similar outbreaks of worship in countries such as England, Sweden, and Canada—that is noncontrived, spontaneous outbreaks of God's people responding to His presence with great joy and enthusiasm. We need to relearn that enthusiasm, the enemy of dignity, means "in God," while dignity means "self-possession."

In January of 1995, while waiting on the Lord for direction for the new year, I experienced the following vision: I saw a huge wheat field with fully mature wheat as far as the eye could see in every direction. The sunlight, symbolic of the Lord's favor, shone softly on the fields. It was more the cool of the day rather than high heat. A gentle breeze, symbolic of the Holy Spirit, was rippling the wheat.

In the midst of the fields was a young girl between 19 and 21 years of age. She was dressed in a beautiful, flowing white dress, such as Revelation 19:8 suggests. She was dancing beyond what any ballet dancer could do. There was no stumbling or hesitancy in her movements, and her leaps and pirouettes were powerful and the very definition of grace. As she was dancing, she actually was holding a scythe and working the harvest.

Realizing that this was picture of the Church at work, I asked the Lord two questions: First, where does this sort of grace come from to be able to dance like this? He responded that "the body has learned to work together rather than apart"— as we so often seem to be in our endless fractions (see Jn. 17:23). Second, where does this sort of strength come from to enable these leaps and pirouettes? He answered, "My joy has become her strength" (see Neh. 8:10).

Toward the outward parts of the picture, many angels watched with joy and amazement as a transformed and healed Church worked. The Lord spoke to the angels in joy over His betrothed. He said, "This is my Bride; isn't she beautiful!"

By making the pursuit of knowledge primary, and worship and prayer a very distant second, we love our doctrines and practices more than the person of God. The greatest commandment—that of loving the Lord our God with all our hearts—can be reduced to a law or theology with very little reality. The heart knowledge of Romans 14:17—"For the kingdom of God is...righteousness, peace and joy in the Holy Spirit"— can be reduced to little more than a teaching. God in the Nineties very much wants to remind us that *He is love* and that the Father sent the Son for the purpose of, life, and life abundantly. In short, Jesus is romancing His Bride!

Appendix A

A Brief, Biblical Look at Five
Manifestations of the Holy Spirit

by Dave Hoffman and Marc Dupont

In February of 1994, the Lord Jesus poured out His Holy Spirit upon Foothills Christian Fellowship, a non-denominational, charismatic church in Southern California. Over a seven-week period, the church held extended evening meetings five nights a week. Many became Christians and others recommitted their lives to Christ, had bondages broken, experienced emotional and physical healings, or simply were spiritually renewed in their lives.

During this outpouring, five distinguishing manifestations of the Holy Spirit as He ministered to individuals were noted. Many people asked, "Why all the shaking, laughing, weeping, and falling over? I just don't understand it! Is there biblical support for what we see taking place?"

The following is a biblical response to these questions, prepared by Foothills' pastor, Dave Hoffman, and edited by myself.

Balanced Discernment: Bible Knowledge, Spiritual Discernment, and Knowing a Little Church History

I do not believe we can ever provide unquestionable, biblical proof texts to support what God has been doing. For example, you will not find a Scripture that says, "As we prayed for them, their bodies began to shake and some fell over. Go, and do likewise."

As I studied this matter, it became apparent that all the manifestations we are experiencing are mentioned in the Bible. Are these manifestations biblical? I would have to say an emphatic "Yes!" Are there specific proof texts for each manifestation? My response: "No!"

Much of what we consider good discernment is dependent on not only having a good knowledge of the Bible but a close relationship with the Holy Spirit. Jesus said in the Gospel of John that the Holy Spirit will "guide you into all the truth...and will disclose to you what is to come" (Jn. 16:13). Proverbs 3:5 instructs us not to lean on our own understanding, but to trust in the Lord with all our hearts.

In First Corinthians, Paul warns that the natural mind cannot understand or apprehend the things of the Spirit (see 1 Cor. 2:14). At the same time, it is valid to ask theological questions and to pursue knowledge of the truth, as long as we keep in mind there is a difference between knowing about the truth and actually knowing the Truth Himself, who will truly lead us, guide us, and give us discernment.

It should be noted that in past outpourings and revivals in America, there have been varied physical manifestations. Jonathan Edwards was perhaps the most outstanding theologian in American history, greatly used by God in the "Great Awakening" (a powerful revival during 1740-1745). In *Account of Revival of Religion in Northampton, 1740-1742*, he writes about the effect of God's Spirit upon people: "It was a very frequent thing to see outcries, faintings, convulsions and such like, both with distress and also admiration and joy."

Though manifestations often accompany the Spirit's outpouring, we should also remember that our emphasis must not be on outward signs, but on the internal work of the Holy Spirit. Many who have come for prayer have exhibited no outward manifestation at all; yet they have experienced tremendous touches from our Lord Jesus.

The Manifestations

1. Trembling or Shaking

A host of Scriptures in the Bible speak about individuals trembling or shaking out of fear, awe, or terror. But we need to understand that in many of these passages the shaking is an involuntary reaction to the overwhelming, manifest presence—as opposed to the omnipresence—of the Lord. Many passages speak about the heavens or earth trembling, whole armies shaking, nations shaking, trees shaking, and so forth, but for our purposes, let us start with Jeremiah:

"Do you not fear Me?" declares the Lord. "Do you not tremble in My presence?" (Jeremiah 5:22).

Here God seems to indicate His people will tremble when in His manifest presence.

Worship the Lord with reverence, and rejoice with trembling (Psalm 2:11).

Here God seems to indicate that while worshiping Him, one might possibly be overcome by His manifest presence.

According to the Scriptures, respectable individuals sometimes experienced trembling when they heard words from the Lord or came into His manifest presence:

I heard and my inward parts trembled, at the sound my lips quivered...and in my place I tremble... (Habakkuk 3:16).

In Acts, we are told that Moses shook in the presence of the Lord (Acts 7:32).

Daniel trembled on his hands and knees when God touched him, and when he stood up, he was still trembling, according to his own account in Daniel 10:8-10.

Scriptural evidence, then, supports the possibility of God's power being so great as to override our faculties to the point of causing trembling or shaking when we encounter the manifest presence of God.

Some still object to the shaking, saying, "I don't understand it; it serves no purpose."

To those I would say, "Since when did man's understanding determine what God would do?" Just think of the cross. No one understood it. Do you think any of Jesus' followers saw God's hand in the arrest and crucifixion of Jesus before His resurrection? Our intellectual understanding should never be used as the sole criteria for determining what is of God.

I have heard others say, "Why would God manifest Himself in such a way as to scare people off? This just doesn't feel like God! God is a God of order, not of confusion!" My dear reader, manifestations of God scare people simply because they are from God.

Many have decided for themselves what God can and cannot do, because they are comfortable with their designated parameters for God. They really do not want a God who is in control and sovereign. They want to have control, so they draw back from sovereign demonstrations of God. Simply put, if God's presence causes a person to tremble and shake, then we should bless it!

2. Falling Over or "Slain in the Spirit"

I like what one man said when asked why individuals fall over when the Holy Spirit comes upon them. He said, "People fall over simply because they cannot stand up!" Or as one theologian has put it, "I did not so much fall down, but as the Lord's presence came over me, up came the floor!"

We have observed over the last months that when God's power overcomes some people, they fall to the ground and occasionally are unable to get up for long periods of time. Such examples can also be found in the Bible.

We are told in First Kings that the priests "could not stand to minister" because God's presence filled the Temple (see 1 Kings 8:11). The word "stand" in Hebrew is *amad* and means "to stand up." If they could not stand, what was happening to them? I believe they were falling over because God's power enveloped them.

Many Scriptures seem to indicate that when experiencing the Lord's presence or hearing His voice, individuals fell down: Genesis 17:3; Leviticus 9:24; Numbers 16:45; Joshua 5:14; Judges 13:20; 1 Kings 18:39; 1 Chronicles 21:16; 2 Chronicles 20:18; Daniel 8:17; Daniel 10:8-10; Matthew 17:6; Revelation 1:17; 4:10; 7:11; 11:16; 22:8.

Some may argue that these individuals who fell on their faces before God or after hearing His voice were merely doing so out of respect and awe, or simply because they were terrified. This may be true for many of the Scriptures but not for all of them, especially when you look at passages like First Kings 8:11 or Daniel 10:8-10, for instance. Ezekiel, the prophet, fell over several times in the presence of God (see Ezek. 1:28; 3:23). Ezekiel 44:4 reads: "...I looked, and behold, the glory of the Lord filled the house of the Lord, and I fell on my face." If you are in a church meeting where someone literally falls face down, as Ezekiel describes, you can be sure it was not done on purpose, because if it were not caused by the Holy Spirit it would seriously damage the individual.

The Hebrew word for "fall" or "cast down" is *naphal*. It has a variety of meanings. Let me quote from the *Theological Wordbook of the Old Testament*, (Harris, Archer, Waltke, Bible Moody Institute of Chicago, Ill., 1980, 587): "Besides the common physical action or occurrence, a violent or accidental circumstance is often indicated." In other words, sometimes the falling over is not planned or expected. I believe many times in the Bible, God's people fell to the ground as a physical response to God's overwhelming manifest presence, which by the sheer power radiating from Him, rendered their human faculties senseless.

In Revelation we have an example of John falling over in the presence of Jesus; "And when I saw Him, I fell at His feet as a dead man" (Rev. 1:17a). Both John's account here and Daniel's in Daniel 10:8-10 state that they collapsed because, as dead men, they had no self-control left to themselves.

In the Garden of Gethsemane, the soldiers who had come to arrest Jesus drew back and fell to the ground when He identified Himself (see Jn. 18:6).

There are also Scriptures that tell us people are thrown to the ground by demons when they manifest. If a mere demon can cause that reaction with some people, it stands to reason that the manifest presence of God can and would do much more, although the fruit obviously would be radically different (see Mk. 3:11; 9:20; Lk. 8:28)!

Note: Many people have been the victims of well-meaning charismatic or Pentecostal ministers who have been heavy-handed. These people end up being pushed by man rather than being overcome by the Spirit. Usually this is the result of over-zealousness on the part of those ministers who, because of poor rolemodeling, carelessly (for the most part), feel they are helping God out. The main problem seems to be people and ministers who seek after an experience, rather than the Lord. These misguided ministers fail to allow God to do exactly what He wants, how He wants, and when He wants. Just as there are people who preach the gospel with false motives, you cannot throw out the baby with the bath water. There has never been a move of God, this side of Heaven in which the flesh of man and the counterfeit presence of the enemy has not been at least a little bit in evidence. We forget that even in Heaven itself there has been rebellion! So to claim that a move is not valid because there are some "flesh" and problems is in itself an invalid argument.

3. Weeping and Crying

We have noticed that one of the most common manifestations of the Holy Spirit's presence is weeping. Weeping has been a part of every revival that has occurred in the United States. Jonathan Edwards, D.L. Moody, and Charles Finney all spoke of people who were so overtaken by God that they broke down and wept.

I would remind the reader that countless people weep when they come to the altars of our churches every Sunday. Whether it is because of the pain they feel, the sin and guilt they carry, or the joy of knowing God has forgiven them and loves them, weeping is a regular experience of many at our worship services.

Scripture is full of passages that connect a humbling and repentant heart with weeping: Joel 2:12,17; Judges 20:26; 21:2; 2 Kings 22:19; Ezra 10:1; 2 Chronicles 34:27; Nehemiah 8:9.

There are even passages of Scripture where the Lord calls or commands His people to weep: "Therefore in that day the Lord...called you to weeping..." (Is. 22:12; see also Joel 2:12-17; Jas. 4:9).

In the Gospel of Luke, Jesus call blessed those who weep (Lk. 6:21).

In Nehemiah, we are told that the people wept when they heard the words of the law (Neh. 8:9).

There are examples of God's people weeping when they came "before Him." "So the people came to Bethel [the house of God] and sat there before God until evening and lifted up their voices and wept bitterly" (Judg. 21:2). For further reading, see Judges 20:23; 20:26 and Luke 7:38.

Many times weeping is also an indication that God is touching someone. The tears and grieving seem to heal a deep hurt or to minister love and forgiveness in a person's life. It is my belief that weeping occasionally can be a part of the normative walk with God until we are with our Lord in Heaven.

4. Stumbling, Rocking Back and Forth, or "Drunk in the Spirit"

As Jeremiah prophesied concerning Judah, he said these words: "...I have become like a drunken man, even like a man overcome with wine, because of the Lord and because of His holy words" (Jer. 23:9). It has been very common to see those who are filled with God's Spirit during this visitation try to preach, teach, or lead the meetings; they are overcome "like drunken men," unable to speak, walk, or stand.

On the day of Pentecost, the Holy Spirit was poured out upon those early believers. They must have been acting like men and women drunk with wine, otherwise we would not have the following passage:

Some, however, made fun of them and said, "They have had too much wine." Then Peter stood up with the Eleven, raised his voice and addressed the crowd: "Fellow Jews and all of you who live in Jerusalem, let me explain this to you; listen carefully to what I say. These men are not drunk, as you suppose. It's only nine in the morning!" (Acts 2:13-15 NIV)

At numerous meetings I have looked around at how the Spirit of God was manifesting Himself on people and thought to myself, "If someone were to walk into this meeting not understanding what was happening, they would definitely think we had been drinking or had taken some sort of drug!" The manifestation of being "drunk in the Spirit" in the Book of Acts is the same manifestation we are experiencing today. I, for one say, "Bless You Jesus for Your works among us."

5. Laughing, the Joy of the Lord

As the Holy Spirit has fallen upon people, many have begun to laugh uncontrollably and continue to laugh for some time. It has been very disconcerting for many to see (and hear) people laughing uncontrollably in church. But as I read through the Bible, I find many Scriptures that speak of God's people being filled with joy, laughter, and gladness. We are told there should be joy and gladness in the presence of the Lord.

They will be glad in Thy presence... (Isaiah 9:3b).

In Thy presence is fulness of joy; in Thy right hand there are pleasures forever (Psalm 16:11b).

Thou dost make him joyful with gladness in Thy presence (Psalm 21:6b).

And the disciples were continually filled with joy and with the Holy Spirit (Acts 13:52).

What does it mean to be "continually filled with joy and with the Holy Spirit?" Is it really so far-fetched to believe that the disciples, as they were filled with the joy of the Lord, at times broke out in spontaneous and perhaps uncontrollable laughter?

What a far cry that must have been in comparison to our often dry, boring, overly somber services.

Speaking about those who would eventually come to know the Lord, Isaiah called them "foreigners." He prophesied, "Even those I will bring to My holy mountain, and make them joyful in My house of prayer" (Is. 56:7a). Isaiah also said, "...Joy and gladness will be found in her..." (Is. 51:3). "Her" refers to God's people as the Bride of Christ.

Should we forget that "the joy of the Lord is [our] strength?" (Neh. 8:10), or that we have been anointed with the oil of gladness (Heb. 1:9) and the oil of joy (Ps. 45:7)?

Laughing may not be common in our churches in North America, but this is certainly nothing to brag about! If the Holy Spirit wants to fill an individual with "joy unspeakable," and it causes that person to laugh, then who are we to call that experience unholy, out of order, or not from the Lord?

Conclusion

In conclusion, there are those who would say about the five manifestations of the Holy Spirit discussed here, "I don't feel good about it; I don't have peace about all this; therefore it can't possibly be from God!" Perhaps these people should re-examine their reasoning, rather than basing their ultimate decision upon feelings. Let us remember the Bible says, "The heart is more deceitful than all else and is desperately sick; who can understand it?" (Jer. 17:9)

Many times people feel comfortable with the status quo and make judgments based solely on personal past experiences (or their lack thereof) and their predetermined spiritual biases. Since Adam and Eve, man has always felt more comfortable trying to intellectually understand God rather than seeking His face and allowing the God whose thoughts are not our thoughts, neither are our ways His ways, to be God in our midst (see Is. 55:8).

My friend, maybe your spiritual grid is wrong. Maybe there really is a spiritual and dynamic encounter with the Holy Spirit that you have never yet experienced. This view is a purely logical assumption, considering that God is so far above us and His ways are so far beyond our understanding (see Is. 55:8-9).

Also, it is inadvisable to use normal church activity as a measuring stick to make judgments on the outpouring of God's Spirit. By its very definition, a revival will result in unusual manifestations and activities.

From a pastoral perspective, the fruit of this outpouring has radically changed people and the whole spiritual atmosphere of our fellowship. Many have testified they have found a new love for and desire to follow our Lord Jesus. We have seen many repent and become Christians as a result of God's power encountering them at one of the meetings. Entire families have turned to the Lord! I truly believe the greatest determining factor of whether or not something is genuinely from God is the fruit it produces (see Jn. 15:4-8).

The fruit from this outpouring has surpassed our expectations, especially in the area of personal prayer, intercession, and daily devotions.

My prayer for our church and all who call upon the name of the Lord is this: "Come, Lord Jesus, fill us again, conform us to Your image. Give us boldness to speak out in Your name, that many may come to the true knowledge of our Savior Jesus Christ."

Appendix B

A few verses that demonstrate some of the effects of God's manifest presence.

Exodus 33:14 (NIV): *The Lord replied, "My **Presence** will go with you, and I will give you rest."*

Leviticus 9:24 (NIV): *Fire came out from the **presence** of the Lord and consumed the burnt offering and the fat portions on the altar. And when all the people saw it, they shouted for joy and fell facedown.*

Deuteronomy 4:37 (NIV): *Because He loved your forefathers and chose their descendants after them, He brought you out of Egypt by His **Presence** and His great strength.*

Deuteronomy 12:7 (NIV): *There, in the **presence** of the Lord your God, you and your families shall eat and shall rejoice in everything you have put your hand to, because the Lord your God has blessed you.*

1 Samuel 6:20 (NIV): *And the men of Beth Shemesh asked, "Who can stand **in the presence** of the Lord, this holy God? To whom will the ark go up from here?"*

2 Samuel 22:13 (NIV): *Out of the brightness of His **presence** bolts of lightning blazed forth.*

2 Kings 22:19 (NIV): *"Because your heart was responsive and you humbled yourself before the Lord when you heard what I have spoken against this place and its people, that they would become accursed and laid waste, and because you tore your robes and **wept in My presence**, I have heard you," declares the Lord.*

1 Chronicles 29:22 (NIV): *They ate and drank with **great joy** in the **presence** of the Lord that day.*

2 Chronicles 34:27 (NIV): *"Because your heart was responsive and you humbled yourself before God when you heard what He spoke against this place and its people, and because you **humbled** yourself before Me and tore your robes and **wept** in My **presence**, I have heard you," declares the Lord.*

Ezra 9:15 (NIV): *O Lord, God of Israel, You are righteous! We are left this day as a remnant. Here we are before You in our guilt, though because of it not one of us can stand in Your **presence**.*

Psalm 16:11 (NIV): *You have made known to me the path of life; You will **fill me with joy** in Your **presence**, with eternal pleasures at Your right hand.*

Psalm 18:12 (NIV): *Out of the brightness of His **presence** clouds advanced, with hailstones and bolts of lightning.*

Psalm 21:6 (NIV): *Surely You have granted him eternal blessings and made him glad with the **joy of Your presence**.*

Psalm 114:7 (NIV): *Tremble, O earth, at the **presence** of the Lord, at the **presence** of the God of Jacob.*

Isaiah 26:17 (NIV): *As a woman with child about to give birth writhes and cries out in her pain, so were we in Your **presence**, O Lord.*

Jeremiah 5:22a (NIV): *"Should you not fear Me?" declares the Lord. "Should you not **tremble** in My **presence**?"*

Lamentations 2:19 (NIV): *Arise, **cry** out in the night, as the watches of the night begin; **pour out your heart** like water in the **presence** of the Lord. **Lift up your hands** to Him for the lives of your children, who faint from hunger at the head of every street.*

Ezekiel 38:20 (NIV): *The fish of the sea, the birds of the air, the beasts of the field, every creature that moves along the ground, and all the people on the face of the earth will **tremble** at My **presence**. The mountains will be overturned, the cliffs will crumble and every wall will fall to the ground.*

Nahum 1:5 (NIV): *The mountains quake before Him and the hills melt away. The earth **trembles** at His **presence**, the world and all who live in it.*

Acts 2:28 (NIV): *You have made known to me the paths of life; You will **fill me with joy in Your presence**.*

1 John 3:19 (NIV): *This then is how we know that we belong to the truth, and how we set our hearts at **rest** in His **presence**.*

D*estiny Image*
Revival Books